READY FOR SEA

READY FOR SEA

A Guide to Systematic Boat Maintenance
Power and Sail

*Basil Mosenthal and
Dick Hewitt*

ADLARD COLES LIMITED
GRANADA PUBLISHING
London Toronto Sydney New York

Published by Granada Publishing in
Adlard Coles Limited 1981

Granada Publishing Limited
Frogmore, St Albans, Herts AL2 2NF
and
3 Upper James Street, London W1R 4BP
Suite 405, 4th Floor, 866 United Nations Plaza, New York,
NY 10017 USA
Q164 Queen Victoria Buildings, Sydney, NSW 2000, Australia
100 Skyway Avenue, Toronto, Ontario, Canada M9W 3A6
PO Box 84165, Greenside, 2034 Johannesburg, South Africa
61 Beach Road, Auckland, New Zealand

ISBN 0 229 11647 7

Printed in Great Britain by
Richard Clay (The Chaucer Press) Ltd,
Bungay, Suffolk

Granada ®
Granada Publishing ®

CONTENTS

I N T R O D U C T I O N

This book consits of check lists, notes and equipment lists. Its purpose is to spell out as simply and briefly as possible all those items which need an owner's attention in order to get the boat well found and properly organised.

THE
SYSTEMATIC
APPROACH

Having an efficient boat needs the systematic attention to a large number of details.

Many of the items involved in maintaining a boat do not need great skill or experience. The important thing is that they should all be attended to. But many owners are busy people, and the function of this book is to provide a very necessary reminder.

The various sections in the book must be checked out systematically and action taken on all items that are relevant. If this is done carefully, most common material problems afloat will be avoided.

USING THE
BOOK

There are two parts. Part I - 'The Well
Found Boat' - is concerned with the way
that the boat is fitted out, because even
the best designed and finest built craft
still need to be properly equipped

Part II - 'The Organised Boat' -
consists of check lists for use on
various occasions to help with the
maintenance and the general running
problems. Those lists which are needed
for frequent reference can be photo-
copied and mounted on cards or boards,
so that these are either available for
reference or can be handed out to crew
members when specific checks are to be
made.

EQUIPMENT
LISTS

There are equipment lists at the end of
several sections in Part I. Except for
items in small print, the equipment is
all considered to be essential for normal
cruising. Experienced owners will
recognise any items not relevant to their
particular boat; less experienced owners
are recommended to carry all the items
unless or until they have a good reason
for doing otherwise.

Equipment for boats is often expensive, and this has been kept in mind. Nevertheless, the best advice is 'Never own a boat which you cannot afford to equip and maintain properly'. Buying cheap and unsuitable equipment or cutting corners in other ways is never satisfactory in the long run and may even be downright dangerous. However, careful maintenance reduces running costs and improves the value of a boat.

Section 10 deals with Sails and Rigging, but all other sections are generally applicable to both power and sail. There will be no problem in recognising items that do not concern a particular boat.

In both parts, the items printed in CAPITALS and indicated by ☐ are those which, where relevant, need to be specifically checked off onboard.

Throughout, 'crew' is used as a convenient term for all those onboard - not only those involved in actively sailing the boat.

OWN BOAT DATA   It is not possible to run or maintain a boat efficiently unless everything about her and her gear is known and (preferably) recorded. A modern boat of even modest size can be so complex that it is impossible for the owner to remember all the details about her, and often quite basic information is not available when wanted. Such details as the part number of the engine fuel filters, the capacity of the batteries, or the size of the main halyard may not be needed every day, but the information should be readily obtainable.

There is a section at the end of the book, printed in italics, for recording details of the reader's own boat. In this way they will be easy to locate at any time.

PART I

PART I   THE WELL FOUND BOAT

Many of the things that go to making a
boat well found are designed and built
into her, and if a boat has been poorly
designed, badly built, or seriously
neglected, there may not be much that can
be done to improve her. However, the
assumption here is that we are dealing
with a fundamentally sound vessel.

The Check Lists and Equipment Lists
in this part of the book show the items -
both major and minor - which help to make
a boat well found. Small details are
important. Once the basic matters have
been taken care of, it is the small
details which will finally achieve safety
and efficiency onboard. It is quite easy
to envisage a dangerous situation
developing just because of the lack of a
simple tool or spare part, or because an
elementary piece of maintenance has been
overlooked.

SECTION 1   DECK CHECK

ANCHOR GEAR

☐ 1.1 THERE ARE AT LEAST TWO ANCHORS, OF WHICH ONE MAY BE A SMALLER KEDGE. For serious cruising two bower or working anchors plus a kedge are better.

☐ 1.2 THE SIZE OF THE ANCHORS IS ADEQUATE. See recommended sizes (see 1.40).

☐ 1.3 THERE ARE AT LEAST TWO ANCHOR LINES AND/OR ANCHOR CHAINS OF SUFFICIENT SIZE AND LENGTH. There may be one of each. See recommended sizes (see 1.40).

☐ 1.4 IF THE ANCHOR LINE IS ROPE, THERE IS AT LEAST 3 FATHOMS (5 METRES) OF CHAIN BETWEEN THE LINE AND THE ANCHOR. This is optional for the kedge anchor, although a short length of chain is still desirable.

☐ 1.5 THE SHACKLE SECURING THE CHAIN TO THE ANCHOR IS MOUSED WITH WIRE TO PREVENT UNDOING.

☐ 1.6 THE INBOARD END OF THE ANCHOR LINE OR CHAIN IS SECURED. This should be done with a lashing which can be cut if the cable has to be slipped.

ANCHOR
GEAR
(cont'd)

☐ 1.7 ANCHOR CHAIN AND LINE ARE MARKED AT
REGULAR INTERVALS (SAY EVERY 5 FATHOMS OR
10 METRES). (This saves guesswork).
Chain can be marked with wire seizings,
but painted marks (which need occasional
renewal) are easier to see. Lines can be
marked with plastic markers inserted in
the lay of the rope.

☐ 1.8 THE CHAIN PIPE, OR ANY OTHER ACCESS
FROM THE DECK TO THE CABLE LOCKER OR
FOREPEAK, HAS A WATERTIGHT COVER FOR USE
AT SEA AND DURING HEAVY RAIN.

☐ 1.9 ANCHORS ARE WELL SECURED AT SEA,
INCLUDING A LASHING OR A SUITABLE
SECURING DEVICE ON ANY ANCHOR PERMANENTLY
STOWED IN A BOW FAIRLEAD.

☐ 1.10 ANY ANCHOR STOWED BELOW CAN BE
BROUGHT TO THE DECK WITH REASONABLE EASE
BY THE NORMAL CREW.

☐ 1.11 BOW ROLLER OR FAIRLEAD
       - DOES PROVIDE A FAIR LEAD TO THE
CHAIN OR LINE WHEN WORKING THE ANCHOR
       - HAS A PIN OR COVER TO PREVENT THE
CHAIN OR LINE FROM JUMPING OUT.

ANCHOR
GEAR
(cont'd)

☐ 1.12 THE ANCHOR WINDLASS, IF FITTED, IS
BOLTED THROUGH TO A PAD BENEATH THE DECK
AND IS COMPLETELY SECURE.

☐ 1.13 WITH AN ANCHOR WINDLASS, THERE IS A
PAWL OR SIMILAR ARRANGEMENT TO PREVENT
ALL THE WEIGHT OF THE CHAIN RESTING ON
THE WINDLASS BRAKE WHEN AT ANCHOR.

☐ 1.14 WHEN NO WINDLASS IS FITTED, THERE IS
A CLEAT OR SAMSON POST, WELL SECURED AND
OF SUFFICIENT SIZE TO TURN UP THE ANCHOR
LINE OR CHAIN SAFELY AND EASILY.

☐ 1.15 WHEN UNDER WAY IN RESTRICTED WATERS,
AN ANCHOR CAN BE LET GO QUICKLY IN THE
EVENT OF ENGINE OR STEERING BREAKDOWN OR
OTHER EMERGENCY. An anchor not only
tethers you to the ground but acts as a
brake in emergency.

DECK
GEAR

☐ 1.16 THERE ARE ENOUGH FENDERS ONBOARD TO
UPHOLSTER THE BOAT IN ANY NORMAL BERTH.
Six should be the minimum. About 10 in.
(250 mm) diameter is a good size for a
30 ft (9 metre) boat. Fenders should be
able to hang vertically or horizontally
according to where the boat is lying.

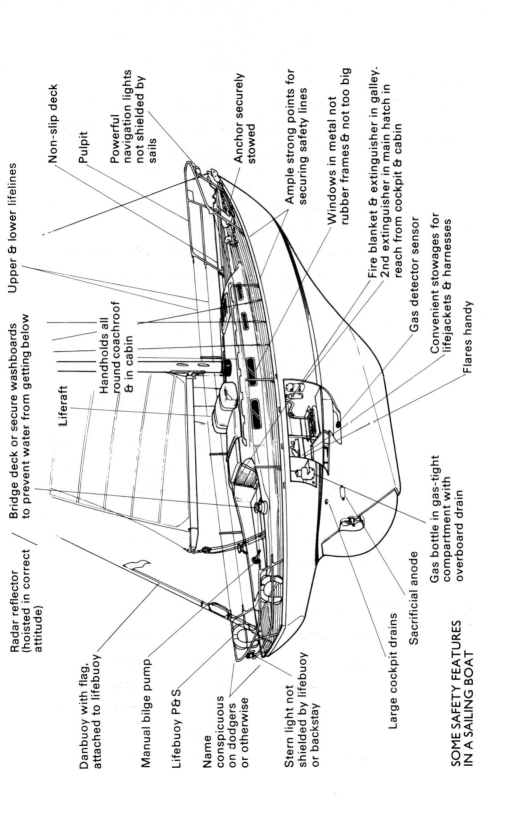

Radar reflector
(hoisted in correct
attitude)

Bridge deck or secure washboards
to prevent water from getting below

Upper & lower lifelines

Non-slip deck

Pulpit

Powerful
navigation lights
not shielded by
sails

Anchor securely
stowed

Ample strong points for
securing safety lines

Windows in metal not
rubber frames & not too big

Fire blanket & extinguisher in galley.
2nd extinguisher in main hatch in
reach from cockpit & cabin

Gas detector sensor

Convenient stowages for
lifejackets & harnesses

Flares handy

Liferaft

Handholds all
round coachroof
& in cabin

Danbuoy with flag,
attached to lifebuoy

Manual bilge pump

Lifebuoy P&S

Name
conspicuous
on dodgers
or otherwise

Stern light not
shielded by lifebuoy
or backstay

Large cockpit drains

Sacrificial anode

Gas bottle in gas-tight
compartment with
overboard drain

SOME SAFETY FEATURES
IN A SAILING BOAT

DECK
GEAR
(cont'd)

☐ 1.17 THERE ARE SUFFICIENT MOORING LINES OF THE RIGHT SIZE. At least <u>six</u> are needed. See recommended sizes and lengths (1.43).

☐ 1.18 IN ADDITION TO THE MOORING LINES, THERE IS AT LEAST ONE LONG LINE (SAY 100 ft OR 30 metres) FOR TOWING, BEING TOWED, ETC.

☐ 1.19 CLEATS ARE BOLTED THROUGH THE DECK. THEY ARE OF SUFFICIENT SIZE TO HANDLE THE MOORING LINES EASILY, AND ARE CONVENIENTLY SITED IN RELATION TO THE FAIRLEADS.

APPEAR-
ANCE

☐ 1.20 THE STOWAGE FOR DECK GEAR IS ORGANISED SO THAT:

- FENDERS AND LINES CAN BE SECURELY STOWED AT SEA.
- UNUSED GEAR CAN BE (AND IS) STOWED AWAY WHEN IN PORT, LEAVING THE DECKS TIDY AND SHIPSHAPE.

☐ 1.21 ENSIGN, BURGEE, AND OTHER FLAGS ARE NOT FADED OR FRAYED, AND ARE PROPERLY HOISTED WITH THE HALYARDS HAULED TAUT. A smart appearance is badly spoiled by shabby and incorrectly hoisted flags.

☐ 1.22 LIFELINE STANCHION BASES ARE BOLTED THROUGH THE DECK - NOT SCREWED.

☐ 1.23 LIFELINE STANCHIONS ARE, WHERE APPROPRIATE, SECURED WITH PINS INTO STANCHION BASES.

☐ 1.24 THERE ARE TWO LIFELINES - UPPER AND LOWER - AND THE MINIMUM HEIGHT OF THE TOP LIFELINE IS 2 ft (0.6 metres).

☐ 1.25 THERE ARE NO SLIPPERY AREAS ON DECK, PARTICULARLY WHERE THE CREW MAY HAVE TO WORK, SUCH AS THE TOP OF THE COACHROOF OR AROUND THE MAST IN A SAILING YACHT.

☐ 1.26 THE LIFELINES AND THE STANCHIONS ARE SUFFICIENTLY STRONG TO SUPPORT THE WEIGHT OF A HEAVY PERSON VIOLENTLY THROWN AGAINST THEM. When inspecting wire lifelines, their potential weak points are likely to be where they pass through the stanchions, and at either end adjacent to the fittings. Catches and latches on wooden rails must work efficiently.

SAFETY ☐ 1.27 THERE ARE SUFFICIENT HANDHOLDS, PARTICULARLY ROUND A DECKHOUSE OR SUPERSTRUCTURE SO THAT IT IS POSSIBLE TO GO FORWARD AND OTHERWISE MOVE AROUND THE DECK IN SAFETY.

☐ 1.28 IN A SAILING YACHT THERE ARE SUFFICIENT PLACES WHERE A SAFETY HARNESS CAN BE HOOKED ON, ESPECIALLY FOR THOSE SITTING IN THE COCKPIT OR MAKING THEIR WAY TO THE FOREDECK. It should be possible for a person to be hooked on before emerging into the cockpit.

YACHT
TENDERS -
DINGHIES
AND
INFLATABLES ☐ 1.29 Dinghies are likely to be the source of far more insurance claims than their parent yachts, and these craft need more attention than they often get.

☐ 1.30 FIBREGLASS OR WOODEN DINGHY HAS SUFFICIENT BUILT-IN OR WELL SECURED BUOYANCY TO SUPPORT HERSELF AND HER PASSENGERS, SHOULD SHE BECOME SWAMPED.

☐ 1.31 ALL TENDERS HAVE SOUND BOW AND STERN PAINTERS. AT LEAST 16 ft (5 metres) IS A USEFUL LENGTH, AND THEY SHOULD BE LONGER IN AREAS WITH A LARGE TIDAL RISE AND FALL.

YACHT
TENDERS
(cont'd)

☐ 1.32 IN A FIBREGLASS OR WOOD DINGHY, THE BOW PAINTER IS SECURED TO AN EYEBOLT BOLTED THROUGH THE STEMHEAD.

☐ 1.33 ROWLOCKS OR OARLOCKS ARE FITTED WITH LANYARDS OR OTHERWISE SECURED SO THAT THEY CANNOT BE LOST. The type of closed rowlock that holds an oar so that it cannot be lost over the side is strongly recommended.

☐ 1.34 A BAILER IS ALWAYS CARRIED AND A WATER PROOF FLASHLIGHT AT NIGHT.

☐ 1.35 OARS OR PADDLES ARE ALWAYS CARRIED IN ADDITION TO AN OUTBOARD MOTOR.

☐ 1.36 THE PARENT VESSEL'S NAME IS SHOWN ON THE TENDER.

☐ 1.37 THE OUTBOARD MOTOR IS FITTED WITH A LANYARD WHICH IS SECURED TO PREVENT AN ACCIDENT WHEN THE MOTOR IS LOWERED INTO THE TENDER: THEN SECURED AS AN ADDITIONAL SAFEGUARD WHEN THE MOTOR IS IN THE BOAT.

☐ 1.38 OUTBOARD MOTOR FUEL IS STOWED ON DECK. Never below decks.

YACHT
TENDERS
(cont'd)

1.39   FOR LONGER TRIPS:

- A BOAT'S ANCHOR AND 50 ft (15 metres) OF LINE.

- SPARE FUEL.

- SPARE SHEAR PIN, SPLIT PIN, AND PLIERS.

ANCHOR GEAR - 1.40
RECOMMENDED SIZES

Overall length of boat		Working anchor		Kedge anchor		Anchor chain diameter		Anchor warp (nylon)		
ft	m	lbs	kg	lbs	kg	in	mm	diam in	mm	circ in
25	8	22	10	15	7	1/4	6.3	1/2	12	1½
30	9	30	14	22	10	5/16	8	9/16	14	1¾
35	11	40	19	22	10	5/16	9.5	9/16	14	1¾
40	12.5	40	19	30	14	3/8	9.5	9/16	14	1¾
45	13.5	50	25	35	16	3/8	9.5	5/8	16	2
50	15	50	25	40	19	7/16	11.2	5/8	16	2

Notes:

1.   Anchor sizes refer to Danforth type or CQR anchors. For Fisherman anchors multiply by at least two.

2.   Boats of heavy displacement or carrying out extended cruises, and those which anchor frequently in unsheleterd waters, should carry heavier gear. By

ANCHOR GEAR
(cont'd)
the same token, boats used only in sheltered inshore waters need rather less. But, provided it can be handled, substantial ground tackle gives an owner both added security and peace of mind.

AMOUNT OF
ANCHOR LINE
TO CARRY
1.41 Anchor line should be seven times the maximum depth in which it is expected to anchor. 50 fathoms (90 metres) is suggested. Anchor line should be nylon.

AMOUNT OF
CHAIN TO
CARRY
1.42 The normal chain requirement is not less than five times the maximum depth in which it is expected to anchor. Less chain can be used in fine weather. 35 fathoms (65 metres) is a good length for most yachts.

MOORING
LINES
1.43 Same diameter as anchor line, but normally of polyester. Two different lengths are convenient, and for a 30 ft (9 metre) boat three 30 ft (9 metre) and three 20 ft (6 metre) lines are suggested. It is also desirable to carry one other longish heavy duty line for towing, being towed, or other general purposes - say 100 ft (30 metres).

1.44 <u>DECK EQUIPMENT LIST</u>

- [ ] ANCHORS
- [ ] ANCHOR CHAIN OR LINES
- [ ] LONG LINE FOR KEDGING ETC
- [ ] MOORING LINES
- [ ] FENDERS
- [ ] BOAT HOOK
- [ ] SWIMMING/BOARDING LADDER
- [ ] ANCHOR LIGHT
- [ ] ANCHOR SHAPE AND MOTOR-SAILING CONE
- [ ] HEAVING LINE
- [ ] KEYS FOR WATER AND FUEL FILLING CAPS

- [ ] ENSIGN
- [ ] ENSIGN STAFF
- [ ] BURGEE

DINGHY:
- [ ] OARS
- [ ] ROWLOCKS/OARLOCKS
- [ ] ANCHOR & LINE

- [ ] SCRUBBER
- [ ] MOP
- [ ] SPONGE
- [ ] PLASTIC BUCKET
- [ ] LEATHER CLOTH

- [ ] BAILER
- [ ] PAINTERS
- [ ] BELLOWS & REPAIR KIT (INFLATABLE)

Cockpit and Deck cushions

Wheel and winch covers

Cockpit spray dodgers (weather cloths)

Hatch covers

Fresh water hose

For deck tools etc see 9.7

SECTION 2   HULL CHECK

SEACOCKS ☐ 2.1 SEACOCKS - VALVES MOVE FREELY BY
ETC.   HAND. FASTENINGS LOOK SOUND, AND THERE IS
             NO SIGN OF CORROSION ON FASTENINGS OR
             FLANGES.

          ☐ 2.2 ALL THROUGH-HULL FITTINGS ARE
             ACCESSIBLE FOR OPERATION & MAINTENANCE.

          ☐ 2.3 ALL THROUGH-HULL FITTINGS NEAR OR
             BELOW THE WATERLINE ARE FITTED WITH
             SEACOCKS.

          ☐ 2.4 ANY FLEXIBLE PIPING IS SECURED TO
             THROUGH-HULL FITTINGS WITH DOUBLE HOSE
             CLIPS. Stainless steel clips are safest.

STERN   ☐ 2.5 STERN GLANDS ETC. ARE ACCESSIBLE FOR
GLANDS   ADJUSTMENT AND MAINTENANCE.

          ☐ 2.6 TOOLS ARE AVAILABLE FOR THE ADJUST-
             MENT OF THE STERN GLAND AND THE RUDDER
             POST GLAND IF REQUIRED. These fittings
             may need larger tools than normal.

HATCHES   ☐ 2.7 RUBBER GASKETS ON HATCHES AND PORTS
AND PORTS   ARE SOUND (NOT PAINTED), FASTENINGS WORK
             EFFICIENTLY AND SCREW THREADS LUBRICATED.
             WASHBOARDS ARE LOCKABLE.

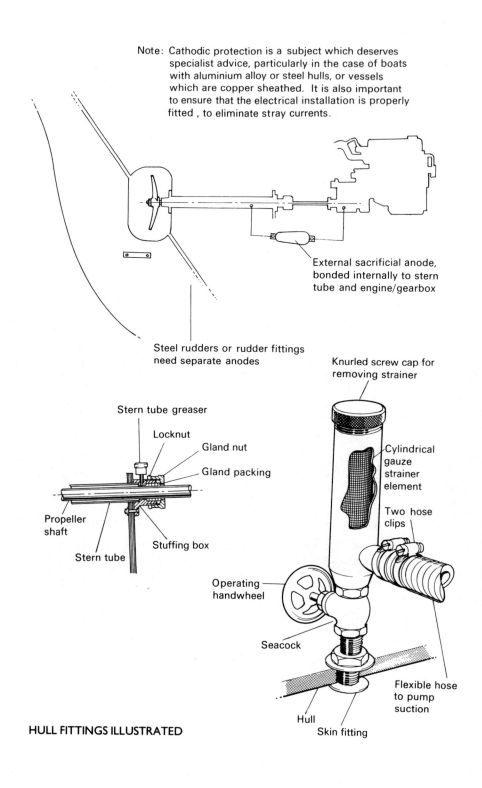

Note: Cathodic protection is a subject which deserves
specialist advice, particularly in the case of boats
with aluminium alloy or steel hulls, or vessels
which are copper sheathed. It is also important
to ensure that the electrical installation is properly
fitted , to eliminate stray currents.

External sacrificial anode,
bonded internally to stern
tube and engine/gearbox

Steel rudders or rudder fittings
need separate anodes

Knurled screw cap for
removing strainer

Stern tube greaser

Locknut

Gland nut

Gland packing

Cylindrical
gauze
strainer
element

Two hose
clips

Propeller
shaft

Stern tube

Stuffing box

Operating
handwheel

Seacock

Flexible hose
to pump
suction

Hull

Skin fitting

HULL FITTINGS ILLUSTRATED

BILGES ☐ 2.8 ALL AREAS OF THE BILGE ARE ACCESS-
IBLE, AND CAN BE EASILY INSPECTED. If
this is not so, corrosion and leaks can
remain undetected, and are difficult to
remedy when they are found.

☐ 2.9 FLOOR BOARDS ARE EASILY REMOVABLE
FOR BILGE INSPECTION.

☐ 2.10 THERE ARE ADEQUATE LIMBER HOLES IN
THE BILGES SO THAT ANY WATER IN THE BILGE
WILL QUICKLY DRAIN TO THE SUMPS WHERE THE
BILGE PUMP SUCTIONS ARE SITED.

☐ 2.11 BILGES ARE GENERALLY CLEAN AND FREE
FROM DEBRIS.

AUTOMATIC ☐ 2.12 Automatic bilge pumps can give
BILGE
PUMPS valuable protection when a boat is
unattended. When the boat is in use
there is a chance than an automatic pump,
doing its job well, may disguise a leak.
There should be an indicator light to
show when the pump is working.

BILGE
PUMPS

☐ 2.13 THERE ARE AT LEAST TWO BILGE PUMPS ONBOARD AND AT LEAST ONE OF THESE IS A MANUAL PUMP. Diaphragm type manual pumps are easier to operate and more efficient than the plunger type. They are also easier to clear if they get blocked.

☐ 2.14 MANUAL BILGE PUMPS
- ARE SITED ABOVE THE WATERLINE.
- ARE FIRMLY SECURED TO THE BOAT'S STRUCTURE (considerable leverage is exerted in operation).
- ARE POSITIONED SO THAT, IF NECESSARY, PROLONGED OPERATION IS POSSIBLE WITH A REASONABLE DEGREE OF COMFORT FOR THE OPERATOR.
- WHEN HANDLE IS REMOVABLE, IT HAS A STOWAGE (USUALLY IN CLIPS) ALONGSIDE THE PUMP AND CANNOT BE LOST.
- ONE PUMP WILL STILL OPERATE WHEN ALL LOCKERS AND HATCHES ARE CLOSED.

☐ 2.15 ALL PUMP SUCTIONS ARE FITTED WITH STRAINERS.

☐ 2.16 SUCTIONS CAN BE REACHED BY HAND SO THAT THEY CAN BE CLEARED IF BLOCKED.

FRESH
WATER
SYSTEM

☐ 2.17 IF A PRESSURE FRESH WATER SYSTEM IS
FITTED, THERE IS ALSO A MANUAL PUMP,
PREFERABLY IN THE GALLEY. This is in
case the electric pump breaks down.   A
salt water back-up for washing dishes
saves tank water.

COCKPITS ☐ 2.18 COCKPIT DRAINS ARE SITED SO THAT
COCKPIT WILL EMPTY ON EITHER TACK, AND
HULL OPENINGS ARE FITTED WITH SEACOCKS.

☐ 2.19 COCKPIT DRAINS ARE OF ADEQUATE SIZE
TO DRAIN COCKPIT QUICKLY. THIS MUST BE
TESTED. Cockpit drains are frequently
too small. The only satisfactory answer
is to fill the cockpit and see how
quickly it drains; 2 - 3 mins is the
target. The IOR rules for yachts over
21 ft (6.1m) rating specify minimum of
four 3/4 in (20 mm) drains (after allowance for screens on the drains); this is
a good guide for all boats.

☐ 2.20 COMPANION WAYS, IF EXTENDED BELOW
THE LEVEL OF THE MAIN DECK, ARE CAPABLE
OF BEING BLOCKED OFF TO THE LEVEL OF THE
MAIN DECK WHILE STILL ALLOWING ACCESS
BELOW. This means that if the cockpit is
flooded, water is prevented from pouring
below.

Section 2

STEERING ☐ 2.21 TILLER IS SOUND AND WELL SECURED.

2.22 WHEEL STEERING - If wheel is
connected to rudder head with cables:

☐ - THE LEAD OF THE CABLES IS KNOWN
IN CASE OF DAMAGE. Steering cables
are often concealed in liners.

☐ - LUBRICATING POINTS, IF ANY, ARE
NOTED. SHEAVES ARE PROTECTED (SO
THAT NOTHING CAN FOUL THE CABLE)
AND BOLTED - NOT SCREWED - INTO THE
ADJACENT STRUCTURE.

☐ - STEERING CABLES ARE SECURED TO
THE QUADRANT OR OTHER RUDDER HEAD
FITTING WITH SWAGED TERMINALS OR
WITH THREE CABLE CLAMPS.

If wheel is connected via torque rods:

☐ - ANY LUBRICATION POINT IS NOTED.

☐ 2.23 THE RUDDER POST IS FREE FROM LEAKS
OR OBVIOUS WEAR.

☐ 2.24 THE AREA ROUND THE RUDDER HEAD
IS SUCH THAT GEAR CANNOT FOUL THE RUDDER.

☐ 2.25 EMERGENCY TILLER HAS BEEN TESTED,
AND CREW KNOW HOW TO RIG AND USE IT.

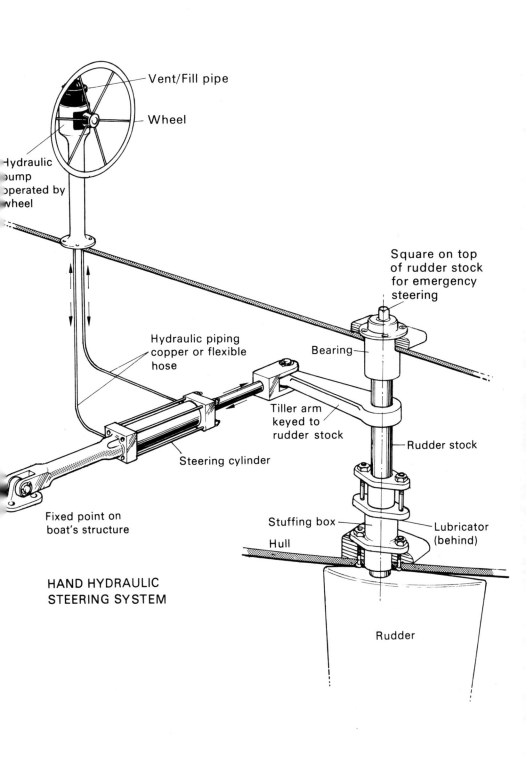

Vent/Fill pipe

Wheel

Hydraulic
pump
operated by
wheel

Square on top
of rudder stock
for emergency
steering

Hydraulic piping
copper or flexible
hose

Bearing

Tiller arm
keyed to
rudder stock

Rudder stock

Steering cylinder

Fixed point on
boat's structure

Stuffing box

Lubricator
(behind)

Hull

**HAND HYDRAULIC
STEERING SYSTEM**

Rudder

SAFETY AND EMERGENCY EQUIPMENT CHECK

There are two requirements here:

(a) Have the right equipment onboard.

(b) Have that equipment properly
    organised, stowed, and maintained.

In the U.K. boats of 45 ft (13.7m) and
over are required by law to carry certain
minimum items of safety equipment -
details in *Reed's Nautical Almanac* and
elsewhere.   There are similar requirements in other countries.

THE RIGHT ☐   3.1 LIFERAFT OR INFLATABLE DINGHY -
EQUIPMENT   carried onboard if cruising other than
                 local waters. (See 3.26).

☐   3.2 LIFEJACKETS - one more than the
      maximum number expected onboard.
      Children's sizes too if needed. (See 3.27)

☐   3.3 SAFETY HARNESS - in a sailing boat,
      one for each member of the crew.   In a
      motor cruiser two for working on deck
      in bad weather. (See 3.28)

☐   3.4 FLARES - a suitable outfit should be
      carried by all vessels. (See 3.29).

☐ 3.5 FIRE EXTINGUISHERS - (See 3.30).

☐ 3.6 LIFEBUOYS - <u>two</u>, preferably horse-shoe type, with drogue and whistle.

☐ 3.7 BUOYANT LIGHT - for sailing offshore or at night, at least one lifebuoy must have a buoyant light (designed for the job) attached to it.

Note: Marker buoys (with pole and flag) for attaching to lifebuoys are mainly carried in sailing yachts going offshore. There is a greater risk of falling over from a sailing yacht, and the lower freeboard makes it harder to see a person in the water.

☐ 3.8 BOARDING LADDER FOR RECOVERY OF A MAN OVERBOARD - this is essential unless other means are available (See 3.31).

☐ 3.9 HEAVING LINE - carried by all vessels and stowed within reach of the helmsman. Apart from being available to throw to a person in the water, a heaving line has many uses such as passing a tow or sending a line to the shore.

THE RIGHT ☐
EQUIPMENT
(cont'd)

3.10 MEDICAL OR FIRST AID KIT - must be carried by all vessels, and suitable to deal with any normal emergency until medical assistance is available. (See 3.32).

☐ 3.11 RADAR REFLECTOR - should be carried by all boats. It should be as large as can be reasonably hoisted and displayed in the 'catch rain' position (not point up).

☐ 3.12 WOODEN PLUGS - a supply of soft wooden plugs should be carried to deal with a broken hull skin fitting or a hole.

☐ 3.13 WIRE CUTTERS - carried by yachts sailing offshore and must be able to cut easily through standing rigging in case of dismasting.

☐ 3.14 FLASHLIGHTS (TORCHES) - an ample supply, and one powerful one, with reserve batteries.

☐ 3.15 LIFERAFT (IF CARRIED) - STOWAGE IS
SECURE FROM DAMAGE OR BEING KNOCKED OVER
ACCIDENTALLY, BUT EASY TO LAUNCH. (See
makers' instructions and 3.26).

☐ 3.16 LIFERAFT - SERVICING IS 'IN DATE'
AND RAFT MARKED WITH BOAT'S NAME. See
Liferafts & Inflatables (3.26).

☐ 3.17 LIFEJACKET STOWAGE - THEY ARE KEPT
CLEAN AND DRY, AND INSTANTLY AVAILABLE -
NOT STOWED UNDER OR BEHIND OTHER GEAR.
Stowage can be on an individual basis so
that each member of the crew stows a
lifejacket with his kit, or there can be
a central well-known stowage for all.

☐ 3.18 LIFEJACKETS ARE INSPECTED AT LEAST
ONCE A YEAR. INFLATABLE LIFEJACKETS ARE
INFLATED TO TEST THEM FOR LEAKS. WHERE
FITTED, EMERGENCY LIGHTS ON LIFEJACKETS
ARE TESTED AND BATTERIES RENEWED
ANNUALLY.

☐ 3.19 SAFETY HARNESS STOWAGE - AS FOR
LIFEJACKETS. But as harnesses need
adjusting to individual sizes, advance
issue to individuals is recommended.

STOWAGE,
ORGANIS-
ATION AND
MAINTENANCE
(cont'd)

☐ 3.2O LIFEBUOYS ARE SECURED WITHIN REACH OF THE HELMSMAN, AND CAN BE QUICKLY RELEASED. Although lifebuoys have to be secured against being washed or knocked overboard, there is a general tendency to make them too secure so that there would be an unacceptable delay in throwing them.

☐ 3.21 FLARE STOWAGE KEEPS FLARES DRY AND PROTECTED FROM DAMAGE, BUT READILY AVAILABLE.

☐ 3.22 FLARES ARE 'IN DATE'. Flares have a life of three years, and they are marked with the date on which their guaranteed life expires. They must be replaced before that date.

☐ 3.23 A FIRE EXTINGUISHER IS SITED IN A DECK LOCKER OR DECKHOUSE IN CASE OF A FIRE BELOW DECKS MAKING IT IMPOSSIBLE TO GET BELOW.

☐ 3.24 FIRE EXTINGUISHER MOUNTING CLIPS OR BRACKETS ARE, IF NECESSARY, GREASED OR LUBRICATED, SO THAT THE EXTINGUISHERS MAY BE WITHDRAWN INSTANTLY.

STOWAGE,
ORGANIS-
ATION AND
MAINTENANCE
(cont'd)

3.25   INSTRUCTIONS FOR PASSING A DISTRESS MESSAGE ARE KEPT NEAR THE VHF OR OTHER RADIO TRANSMITTER.   VHF radio is being used by yachts increasingly and it is a valuable method of calling for assistance if in trouble.   However, it is essential that the correct radio procedure is followed and that, once contact is made, the right information about the vessel's position and the nature of the trouble is passed.   In an emergency the radio might have to be operated by someone with no previous experience.   Under stress, even an experienced operator may be glad of a written reminder of the correct drill. Radio distress procedures are shown in *Reed's Nautical Almanac* or US Coast Guard publications.

LIFE-
RAFTS AND
INFLATABLES

3.26   A liferaft is the ultimate piece of emergency equipment, normally only used in the last resort.   It is expensive, but essential for offshore cruising.   If it is ever needed a liferaft must work, and therefore annual servicing is required - also expensive.

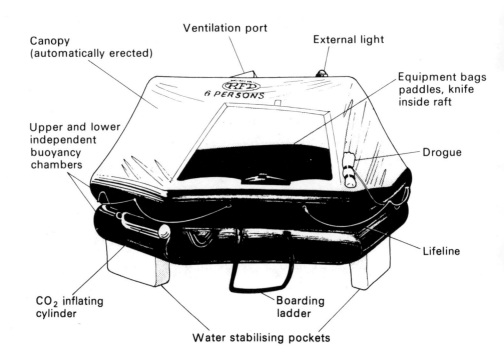

Canopy
(automatically erected)

Ventilation port

External light

Equipment bags
paddles, knife
inside raft

RFD
6 PERSONS

Upper and lower
independent
buoyancy
chambers

Drogue

Lifeline

CO$_2$ inflating
cylinder

Boarding
ladder

Water stabilising pockets

INFLATED LIFERAFT SHOWING SAFETY FEATURES

LIFERAFTS
AND
INFLATABLES
(cont'd)

The liferaft must have sufficient capacity to take all the crew. The contents of the emergency pack must be adequate for the intended type of cruising. The raft should be clearly marked with the name of the boat; this can be done at the annual service.

The raft must be properly mounted/stowed, where it can be got over the side quickly. Launching/inflating instructions should be displayed, and the painter (inflating line) securely fastened to a strong point. All crew members must understand how to launch/inflate the raft, turn it the right way up, and how to get people into it.

An inflatable dinghy (a proper tender, not a beach toy) may be considered a limited alternative to a liferaft in warm weather, and when coastal cruising in waters where help can reasonably be expected within a short time. If such a dinghy is carried on deck, at least one of its compartments should be kept permanently inflated. It is possible to arrange CO_2 inflation.

LIFEJACKETS   3.27 For seagoing, it is essential to have lifejackets which conform to the appropriate standard. These have an established minimum buoyancy and will support the head of an unconscious person with the mouth clear of the water.

For inland waters (rivers, canals etc) a less efficient form of buoyancy aid is acceptable.

Lifejackets should have a whistle made of non-corrosive material, and some have a light that is activated when immersed in water. It is a good idea to fix strips of reflective tape to the collars of lifejackets.

Children and non-swimmers should always wear a lifejacket when afloat, except when down below.

SAFETY   3.28 A safety harness must conform to an
HARNESS   official standard. This should be marked on the harness and looked for when purchasing. The clip is a potential weakness and should always be examined when the harness is inspected.

FLARES   3.29 Officially recommended outfits are:-

Inshore (up to 3 miles from land):

3 red hand flares
2 hand-held orange smoke signals (day use)

Coastal (up to 7 miles from land):

4 two-star signals
4 red hand flares
2 hand-held orange smoke signals (day use)

Offshore (more than 7 miles from land):

4 red parachute rockets
4 red hand flares
2 buoyant orange smoke signals (day use)

The red parachute rockets project a red
flare to a height of about 1000 ft (300
metres): these can be used for raising
the alarm. These rockets have a superior
visibility to the red two-star signals
and, as a boat may quite likely be further
offshore than originally planned, it is
wiser to carry these. Red hand-held
flares will help pin-point the boat's
position for the guidance of the rescuers.

White flares are for drawing attention to a vessel's position (to avoid
collision). They do not indicate distress.
Although not essential, they are useful,
especially in congested waters.

FIRE
EXTINGUISH-
ERS

3.30 Dry powder extinguishers are
officially recommended, and are, perhaps
the most commonly found. However, it can
be difficult to project dry powder
towards a fire in a bilge or other
inaccessible space. BCF or BTM, which
emerge from the extinguisher as gases, are
equally effective and do not have this
disadvantage.

Crews must be aware that this type of
extinguisher can give off dangerous fumes,
particularly if used in a confined space.
For larger engines and engine compartments,
a fixed installation may be advisable.
This will consist of one or more
extinguishers sited in the compartment,
and operated either automatically by a
heat sensor or from a remote control
outside the compartment.

A fire blanket is effective for
galley fires and needs no maintenance.
They are available in containers that
should be mounted within reach of cook or
cockpit.

MAN
OVERBOARD
RECOVERY

3.31 In a man overboard situation, once a lifebuoy has been got to the person in the water and once the boat has reached him, there is still the problem of getting that person onboard. This can be difficult without a strong crew and the problem is often overlooked. One solution is the use of a boarding ladder: either the tubular type normally used for swimming, or a rope ladder with the lowest rung weighted to keep it hanging vertically. In either case, the ladder needs to be stowed on or close to the deck.

This ladder is, of course, just as vital to someone who has fallen from a dinghy or fallen overboard in harbour. In this case, there is available a permanently transom mounted ladder which can be lowered by the person in the water reaching up.

MEDICAL OR
FIRST AID
KIT

3.32 A boat of any size must carry a medical or first aid kit capable of dealing with such accidents as severe cuts, burns, or fingers damaged in winches. These accidents can happen, and a boat can be close inshore and still some time away from medical assistance. Naturally for more extensive cruising, allowance has to be made for dealing with illness as well as injury.

Ready made first aid outfits are convenient for small craft, but it is usually preferable to collect individual items and make up your own outfit. Plastic food containers make an excellent stowage. The list shown below suggests a suitable medical kit for regular coastal and occasional offshore cruising. But there is a large and constantly changing variety of drugs and medicines available and, apart from your own preference, the opinion of your own doctor or a local 'sailing doctor' will be worth having.

MEDICAL KIT   3.33 <u>RECOMMENDED MEDICAL KIT FOR CRUISING</u>

☐ FIRST AID BOOK

☐ BANDAGES –
1", 2" and 4"

☐ BANDAIDS
(larger sizes)

☐ CREPE BANDAGE

☐ VASELINE GAUZE

☐ COTTON WOOL

☐ BUTTERFLY
CLOSURES

☐ ANTISEPTIC
LOTION

☐ SUNBURN LOTION/
CREAM

☐ ANTIBIOTIC
OINTMENT

☐ LAXATIVE

☐ ASPIRIN

☐ TRIANGULAR BANDAGES

☐ ADHESIVE PLASTER

☐ STERILE GAUZE
SQUARES

☐ CLINICAL
THERMOMETER

☐ SURGICAL SCISSORS

☐ SPLINTER FORCEPS

☐ EYE DROPS

☐ CALADRYL/CALAMINE
LOTION

☐ ANTIBIOTIC POWDER

☐ ANTI-DIARRHOEA
REMEDY

☐ SEASICKNESS TABLETS

☐ COUGH MIXTURE OR
TABLETS

Notes:

1. As the most effective remedy for seasickness may be a matter of personal preference, your crew should be encouraged to bring their own - if needed. But a ship's supply should also be carried.

2. There may also be a ready-use supply of bandaids, antiseptic etc available (e.g. in the toilet compartment) so that the crew can attend to minor cuts and scrapes.

SECTION 4   ENGINE CHECK

Most matters concerning the engine(s) are equally applicable to an auxiliary generator. It is important that, if an auxiliary generator is carried, it is checked in the same way as the engine.

GENERAL   ☐   4.1   MANUALS ARE AVAILABLE SHOWING RECOMMENDED PERIODIC MAINTENANCE ROUTINES AND LAY UP PROCEDURES. See 'Engine Maintenance'. (see 4.18).

☐   4.2   RUNNING HOURS ARE RECORDED.

☐   4.3   MAINTENANCE ROUTINES ARE UP-TO-DATE, AND RECORDED.

☐   4.4   ENGINE COMPARTMENT IS CLEAN SO THAT LEAKS, CORROSION, ETC. CAN BE SEEN.

☐   4.5   RUBBER HOSES AND RESILIENT ENGINE MOUNTINGS ARE NOT PAINTED OVER, NOR ARE MAKERS' NAME OR INSTRUCTION PLATES.

☐   4.6   A DRIP TRAY IS SITED UNDER THE ENGINE (WOODEN HULLS) AND THE BILGE OR DRIP TRAY IN ANY BOAT IS KEPT CLEAN AND FREE FROM OIL, WHICH IS A FIRE HAZARD.

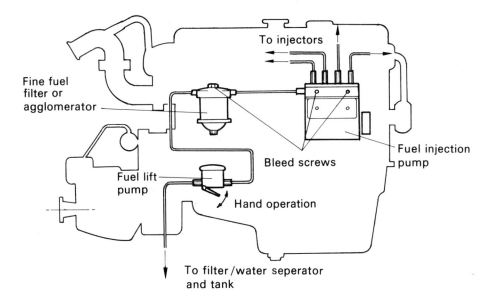

Fine fuel filter or agglomerator

To injectors

Bleed screws

Fuel injection pump

Fuel lift pump

Hand operation

To filter/water seperator and tank

Notes (1) The fuel suction pipe should be clear of the bottom of the tank, which should have a sump where debris can collect and be drained off, and a removable panel for cleaning purposes.

(2) Any filter must be cleaned and have a new element fitted at the recommended interval

DIESEL ENGINE FUEL SYSTEM

Section 4

GENERAL
(cont'd) ☐ 4.7 THERE ARE ARRANGEMENTS FOR EMERGENCY
STARTING. See 'Engine Starting' (see 4.19).

☐ 4.8 ENGINE AND GENERATOR COOLING WATER
INTAKE - SEACOCK WORKS FREELY, AND
STRAINER IS CLEAN AND CAN BE EASILY
REMOVED FOR INSPECTION OR CLEANING WHEN
NEEDED.

☐ 4.9 NORMAL ENGINE OPERATING TEMPERATURES
AND PRESSURES ARE KNOWN AND MONITORED
WHEN UNDER WAY.

☐ 4.10 MAXIMUM PERMISSIBLE RPM FOR
CONTINUOUS RUNNING, AND FOR INTERMITTENT
HIGHER RATING (USUALLY ONE HOUR IN TWELVE),
ARE KNOWN, AND PREFERABLY MARKED ON ENGINE
TACHOMETER. Technical advice may be
needed here.

☐ 4.11 AN RPM/SPEED TABLE IS AVAILABLE.
This is important for navigation.
Information on how to compile the table is
available in many publications.

☐ 4.12 FUEL CONSUMPTIONS AT VARIOUS RPM
HAVE BEEN NOTED, AND ECONOMICAL CRUISING
RPM ARE KNOWN.

GENERAL
(cont'd) ☐

4.13 SUFFICIENT SPARE LUBRICATING OIL FOR AT LEAST A COMPLETE ENGINE OIL CHANGE IS CARRIED ONBOARD. This could be needed in case of a serious oil leak.

☐

4.14 AN ADEQUATE SUPPLY OF TOOLS AND SPARE GEAR, AND MAINTENANCE GEAR IS MAINTAINED ONBOARD. Se Secion 9.

FUEL
SYSTEM ☐

4.15 FUEL PIPING SYSTEM IS KNOWN AND MARKED. Unless it is completely self-evident. (See 4.20).

☐

4.16 FUEL VALVES ARE MARKED, AND EASILY ACCESSIBLE. With more than one tank, it must be generally known onboard how to change tanks. It would also be necessary to cut off fuel in case of fire.

☐

4.17 BLEEDING (VENT) POINTS OF DIESEL FUEL SYSTEMS ARE CLEARLY MARKED. These will be described in the engine manual. It is usually necessary to bleed the fuel system after changing fuel filters. Note that this might have to be carried out as an emergency procedure at sea (if filters become clogged with dirty fuel).

Section 4

ENGINE
MAINTENANCE

4.18 Manufacturers set out maintenance procedures in their handbooks. These vary from daily checking of the lubricating oil and fresh water, to changing of fuel and oil filters every couple of hundred hours or so (or seasonally), and the major overhauls that may become due only every two or three seasons. Additionally, there are winter lay up procedures which are important.

REGULARLY CARRYING OUT THESE ROUTINE PROCEDURES, BOTH MAJOR AND MINOR, IS THE BASIS OF ACHIEVING MAXIMUM RELIABILITY, PERFORMANCE AND LIFE FROM AN ENGINE.

If maintenance is to be carried out after a specific number of hours, then there must be a record of hours run. These are most easily recorded by an engine hour meter which is fitted to many engines and generators. They may also be noted in the log.

Details of engine and generator maintenance and repairs may be noted in the boat's log or in a separate engine or maintenance log. It is important, however, that they be recorded somewhere.

ENGINE
STARTING

4.19 Engine starting is the most important job for batteries. Whatever the electrical layout, there should be a back-up system for starting, unless the engine can be turned by hand.

- With a pair of batteries of the same voltage, one battery should be used as the service battery and one for starting; it should be possible to use them in parallel.

- With twin engines there will be a starting battery for each engine. There should be a parallel switch which allows both batteries to start either engine.

- If engine starting voltage is not the same as the ship's service voltage (eg 12v starting and 24v for service) there should be an emergency arrangement to start the engine from the service battery.

- If there is an auxiliary generator, then the starting battery for the generator must not be the same as the engine starting battery.

Section 4

ENGINE
STARTING
(cont'd)

In all instances above, there should be a back-up if the engine starting battery fails.

Note: The use of jumper cables for emergency starting should be discouraged. There is a risk that the spark caused when jumper cables are used might cause an explosion because of the hydrogen that is released when batteries are charged.

PIPE
MARKING

4.20 Piping systems should be marked with a colour code to make them easy to identify. This can be helpful for maintenance or repairs and for tracing faults in an emergency.

A suitable code is:

Fuel	-	RED
Fuel return (diesel)	-	ORANGE
Bottled gas	-	RED & WHITE
Fresh water	-	BLUE
Salt water	-	GREEN
Sanitary system	-	BROWN

Pipes can either be marked with strips of plastic tape or with paint.

SECTION 5   ELECTRICAL CHECK

BATTERIES   5.1 BATTERY BOXES:

☐   - ARE SECURED SO THAT BATTERY CANNOT
                   SHIFT OR DROP OUT IF INVERTED.

☐   - HAVE WOODEN OR PLASTIC TOPS TO
                   PREVENT TOOLS BEING ACCIDENTALLY
                   DROPPED ACROSS THE TERMINALS.

☐   - ARE LINED WITH PLASTIC OR LEAD IN
                   CASE OF AN ACID LEAK.

☐   - HAVE ADEQUATE VENTILATION TO ALLOW
                   GASES TO ESCAPE WHEN CHARGING.

☐   5.2 BATTERY TERMINALS ARE CLEAN, FREE
               FROM CORROSION, AND THE CABLES TIGHTLY
               SECURE. This is important, especially for
               starting, when a big current is needed.

☐   5.3 DISTILLED WATER AND A BATTERY FILLER
               ARE ON HAND TO ENSURE PROPER BATTERY CARE.

☐   5.4 A HYDROMETER IS AVAILABLE FOR
               CHECKING SPECIFIC GRAVITY. This gives the
               best indication of a battery's charge.

WIRING   ☐   5.5 A.C. SOCKETS ARE GROUNDED (EARTHED).

☐   5.6 THERE ARE FUSES OR CIRCUIT BREAKERS
               IN EACH CIRCUIT AND FOR EACH ITEM.

WIRING
(cont'd)

☐ 5.7 ALL SWITCHES, CIRCUIT BREAKERS, JUNCTION BOXES, ETC ARE LABELLED OR NUMBERED TO FACILITATE TRACING CIRCUITS. A wiring diagram should be available.

☐ 5.8 ALL CABLES ARE CLIPPED TOGETHER AND SECURED AT REGULAR INTERVALS SO THAT THERE ARE NO LOOSE BIGHTS OF WIRE.

☐ 5.9 ALL CABLE JOINTS ARE MADE WITH PROPER CONNECTIONS, AND NOT TWISTED TOGETHER.

Note: In many boats the original wiring has been done to correct standards, but not when new equipment has been added.

☐ 5.10 IF ELECTRIC POWER IS TAKEN FROM THE SHORE WHILE LYING AT A DOCK, THE POWER LEAD IS OF SUFFICIENT SIZE FOR THE MAXIMUM LOAD (WHICH MUST BE KNOWN), AND WATERPROOF PLUGS ARE FITTED. THERE MUST BE A FUSE OR BREAKER IN THE SHORE POWER CIRCUIT.

☐ 5.11 ENGINES, GENERATORS, TANKS, METAL THROUGH-HULL FITTINGS ARE ALL BONDED TO THE SHIP'S EARTH, BOTH FOR SAFETY AND TO PREVENT ELECTROLYSIS.

SECTION 6 NAVIGATION CHECK

COMPASS ☐ 6.1 COMPASS CORRECTED AND RECENTLY
CHECKED.

☐ 6.2 COMPASS DEVIATION CARD AVAILABLE.

6.3 You must be able to rely on the
accuracy of your compass. It should be
swung and adjusted after it is first
installed, after any major alterations,
or after the boat has been laid up for any
long period. This may best be done by a
professional, but the process is not
difficult and is described in many
yachting books. Every opportunity should
be taken to make a rough compass check,
even if this is only by comparing one
heading with a known transit or range.

Take care that portable radios and
other electronic equipment (including
camera exposure meters) are kept away
from the compass, as well as the more
obvious metallic items like tools or
beer cans.

HAND
BEARING
COMPASS

6.4 A hand bearing compass is essential
equipment unless the steering compass can
be used to take bearings. It can also act
as an emergency steering compass. It
could also be used in a liferaft.

55

ORGANISA-☐
TION

6.5 CHART WORKING SPACE IS AVAILABLE - FIXED OR PORTABLE. Navigation consists not only of looking at charts, but of being able to plot courses and positions on them. Therefore, if no fixed chart table is available, some sort of chart working area must be contrived. The size of a folded British Admiralty chart is approximately 28 in x 20½ in (710mm x 520mm); US charts are not standardised, but are similar in size. There are also certain smaller yachtsman's charts.

☐ 6.6 A PROPER STOWAGE FOR CHARTS IS AVAILABLE. It becomes a nuisance trying to work with charts that have been rolled up: they need to be stowed flat. They can be stowed under a bunk mattress.

☐ 6.7 A STOWAGE IS AVAILABLE FOR BOOKS, ERASER, DIVIDERS, RULES, PENCILS, ETC.

☐ 6.8 A SAFE AND CONVENIENT STOWAGE IS AVAILABLE FOR BINOCULARS, STOP WATCHES, PORTABLE RADIO, AND OTHER BREAKABLE ITEMS. Deck stowage for binoculars is useful.

6.9 THE HELMSMAN'S POSITION IS BOTH
COMFORTABLE AND WELL ARRANGED.

- GOOD VISIBILITY.

- GOOD VIEW OF COMPASS.

- WHEEL WITHIN COMFORTABLE REACH.

- SEAT IS COMFORTABLE (FOR LONG
PERIODS IF NEEDED), LEGS ARE
SUPPORTED AND HELMSMAN IS SECURE
IN ROUGH WEATHER.

- IN A SAILING YACHT, THE HELMSMAN
MUST HAVE SUPPORT WHEN THE BOAT IS
HEELED.

- GOOD VIEW OF INSTRUMENTS.

- ENGINE CONTROLS, HORN ETC, TO HAND.

- LIFEBUOY WITHIN REACH TO THROW.

- ELECTRONICS - RADAR, ECHO SOUNDER,
VHF ETC - ARE WITHIN REACH OF
HELMSMAN, BUT CAN ALSO BE USED BY
OTHERS WITHOUT DISTURBING THE
HELMSMAN. With an open cockpit,
electronics must either be protected
against the weather or sited below.
The echo sounder must be visible to
the helmsman on demand.

**FOGHORN
AND BELL**

6.10 Vessels over 40 ft (12 metres) are
required by law to carry a whistle or horn
and a bell, and a vessel of any size,
moving under power (this includes a
sailing boat using her engine) should be
capable of making the sound signals
required by the International Regulations.
Although many motor boats are fitted with
electric horns, the hand-held aerosol type
is handy and by far the most effective.

A bell is required to be rung at
specified intervals when at anchor in fog.
The regulations allow small craft to use
something else to make the same noise
(beating on a stewpan?) but many owners
like to carry a bell.

**LEAD
LINE**

6.11 Depth sounders are convenient and
are often the first piece of electronic
equipment an owner buys. Nevertheless a
lead line is effective, cheap, and never
breaks down: it is useful to carry, even
with a depth sounder onboard. Most ready-
made lead lines are too long; they become
a nuisance to handle and to stow. About
4 or 5 fathoms is all that is needed,
and it can easily be home made.

Section 6

NIGHT
SAILING

6.12 An owner may not plan on sailing
after dark except, perhaps, for an
occasional night passage on his annual
cruise. But any boat may be caught out in
the dark unexpectedly and she should be
prepared for sailing at night. Running
safely and comfortably in the dark means
more than just switching on the
navigation lights. NIGHT SAILING ARRANGE-
MENTS SHOULD BE CHECKED IN HARBOUR, IN
THE DARK. DO NOT WAIT UNTIL YOU ARE
CAUGHT OUT AT NIGHT.

6.13 NAVIGATION LIGHTS COMPLY WITH THE
REGULATIONS. These regulations are a part
of the International Regulations for
Preventing Collisions at Sea and are shown
in *Reed's Nautical Almanac* as well as in
other publications. In fact it is
difficult to check that lights are showing
over precisely the correct arcs or are
visible at the proper range. The most
important thing is to have navigation
light fittings of the correct design. It
will shortly be mandatory for all vessels
to carry light fittings of approved
manufacture.

NAVIGATION LIGHTS FOR BOATS LESS THAN 20m LONG, UNDER WAY

SAILING BOATS UNDER 12m

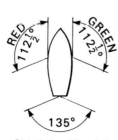 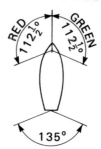 

Sidelights (1 mile) **OR** Combined lantern **OR** Combined three-colour
Sternlight (2 miles)   Sternlight   lantern at masthead

SAILING BOATS 12 - 20m

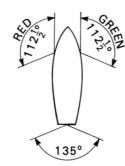 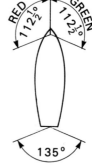

NOTE. ALL LIGHTS ARE WHITE UNLESS SHOWN RED OR GREEN

Sidelights (2 miles) **OR** Combined lantern
Sternlight (2 miles)   Sternlight

Note: A sailing boat under engine must show the appropriate lights for a motor boat

MOTOR BOATS
A: Under 7m and speed under 7 knots
B: Under 12m
C: 12 - 20m

  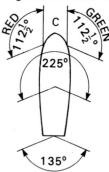

Need only show a white all-round light vis. 2 miles, but if practicable should also show sidelights

Combined lantern (or separate sidelights) vis. 1 mile with masthead light (2 miles) at least 1 metre higher. Sternlight vis. 1 mile

Separate sidelights or combined lantern (2 miles), with masthead lights at least 2.5 metres higher (vis. 3 miles). Sternlight - 2 miles

6.14   NAVIGATION LIGHT FITTINGS ARE
WATERTIGHT. Gaskets on fittings should be
checked, also the glands where the
electric leads enter (which should be
underneath the fitting). Interior of the
fitting should be sprayed with WD40.

6.15   COMPASS LIGHT IS COMFORTABLE
BRIGHTNESS FOR HELMSMAN. Unless the
compass light is fitted with a dimmer, it
is likely to need shading.

6.16   SPARE BULBS FOR COMPASS AND
NAVIGATION LIGHTS ARE ONBOARD.

6.17   INSTRUMENT LIGHTS ARE ADEQUATE, BUT
NOT DISTRACTING FOR THE HELMSMAN. It is
a good arrangement to have the switch
close to the helmsman so that the
instrument lights can be switched off,
except for an occasional check.

Note. The illustration shows the law.
But it will be changed shortly to allow
sailing boats under 20m to use the
combined three colour masthead lantern,
and motor boats under 12m to use a single
all round white masthead light instead of
separate masthead and stern lights.

6.18 CABIN AND OTHER LIGHTS BELOW DECKS ARE SHADED TO AVOID INTERFERENCE WITH VISION ON DECK. In general there will be less need for light at sea than in harbour; but those below decks will still need light to cook, read, etc.

6.19 A 'NIGHT LIGHT' BELOW. On night passages, a well shaded light, sufficient for anyone coming on watch to dress, or for a hot drink to be brewed, is better than either complete darkness or normal light when those below have turned in.

6.20 A WELL SHADED CHART LIGHT. This is important. The skipper or navigator may have to alternate between consulting the chart and keeping a look-out. A pocket flashlight for use with the chart is good.

6.21 A POWERFUL FLASHLIGHT OR SIGNALLING LAMP AND/OR WHITE FLARES ARE READILY AVAILABLE TO THE HELMSMAN IN CASE IT BECOMES NECESSARY TO DRAW URGENT ATTENTION TO THE VESSEL IN ORDER TO AVOID COLLISION.

☐ COMPASS AND DEVIATION CARD
☐ CHARTS
☐ TIDE TABLES
☐ TIDAL ATLAS
☐ REED'S ALMANAC OR EQUIVALENT
☐ PILOT BOOKS OR LOCAL GUIDES

☐ PARALLEL RULERS OR PROTRACTOR
☐ DIVIDERS
☐ PENCILS
☐ ERASER

☐ HAND BEARING COMPASS (See 6.4)
☐ HORN (See 6.10)
☐ BAROMETER
☐ BELL

☐ LEAD LINE (See 6.11)
☐ BINOCULARS
☐ RADIO FOR WEATHER FORECASTS

☐ SPARE BULB FOR COMPASS LIGHT
☐ BULB AND BATTERY FOR HAND BEARING COMPASS
   (depends on type)
☐ BATTERIES FOR RADIO

SECURITY AND
SAFETY BELOW
DECKS

7.1 A major concern below decks - at least from the functional aspect - should be precautions against rough weather and movement of the boat; the matter of keeping things and people in their right places. Even in sheltered waters, the wake of a passing vessel can still cause plenty of movement in a small boat.

☐ 7.2 SUFFICIENT GRAB RAILS ARE SITED NEAR HATCHES, STEPS, AND LADDERS: AND OVERHEAD FOR PASSING THROUGH OPEN AREAS.

☐ 7.3 MOVABLE ITEMS (BOOKS, RADIOS, LAMPS, ASHTRAYS, ETC) ARE EITHER FIXED IN PLACE OR HAVE A SEA STOWAGE THAT IS ALWAYS USED.

☐ 7.4 SHELVES (INCLUDING THOSE INSIDE LOCKERS), TABLES AND WORKING TOPS HAVE EFFECTIVE FIDDLES. Not less than 2 in (50 mm) is a good height. Fiddles on tables should be portable so that they are clear in harbour.

☐ 7.5 ALL DRAWERS AND LOCKER DOORS HAVE POSITIVE CATCHES SO THAT THEY CANNOT FLY OPEN AT SEA.

SECURITY
(cont'd)

☐ 7.6 SHARP CORNERS, SHARP EDGES, AND SPIKY
FITTINGS ARE EITHER ELIMINATED OR PADDED
TO AVOID INJURY.

☐ 7.7 ALL DOORS HAVE CATCHES OR HOOKS SO
THAT THEY CAN BE SECURED IN THE OPEN
POSITION. Apart from saving the
aggravation from slamming doors, this
increases ventilation when the door is not
required to be closed.

☐ 7.8 BERTHS ARE FITTED WITH LEEBOARDS -
WOOD OR CANVAS -- WHICH NOT ONLY HOLD THE
OCCUPANT SAFE BUT WHICH ALSO GIVE A
FEELING OF SECURITY. Leeboards that
'give', even though they may be secure,
are not comfortable.

FOUL
WEATHER
GEAR

☐ 7.9 THERE IS A STOWAGE FOR WET FOUL
WEATHER GEAR AND THE CREW IS MADE TO USE
IT. If there is no locker for foul
weather gear, nor room for one, then the
fo'cs'le or elsewhere should be used.
Small boats become uncomfortable below
decks in bad weather, and wet oilskins (or
any other wet gear) lying around soon
produce a state of squalor.

Section 7

VENTILATION

7.10 Efficient ventilation is important both for comfortable living and for keeping the boat in a sound condition. Detailed arrangements will depend on the type of boat and her lay-out; but, as far as possible, all the following items are desirable.

☐ 7.11 A DODGER TO ALLOW THE FOREHATCH TO REMAIN AT LEAST PARTIALLY OPEN DURING RAIN OR MODERATELY BAD WEATHER.

☐ 7.12 GALLEY WELL SITED FOR MAXIMUM NATURAL VENTILATION, AND ALSO FITTED WITH AN EXTRACTOR FAN OR NATURAL VENT FOR STOVE FUMES.

☐ 7.13 AN EXTRACTOR FAN FITTED IN THE TOILET COMPARTMENT.

☐ 7.14 DOORS AND LOCKERS HAVE VENTILATION OPENINGS. Properly there should be two openings in each door, one high and one low to allow air circulation.

☐ 7.15 ALL DISHES, UTENSILS, FOOD ITEMS OR
WHATEVER DO HAVE A REGULAR AND SECURE SEA
STOWAGE. Galley stowage underway needs
definite planning.

☐ 7.16 GALLEY HAS BEEN DELIBERATELY MADE
EASY TO CLEAN AS FAR AS PRACTICABLE.
Because of the limited space and the
motion, a galley will almost always tend
to get dirtier than a shoreside kitchen,
however careful the cook may be. Easy
cleaning must be deliberately and
thoughtfully built in.

☐ 7.17 IN A SAILING YACHT THERE IS A COOK'S
BELT. This should be a strong, wide belt
secured with spring hooks at either end to
strong pad eyes bolted in place. The cook
should be able to work comfortably and
safely on either tack.

☐ 7.18 THERE ARE FIDDLES AROUND THE TOP OF
THE STOVE, EVEN THOUGH IT MAY BE
GIMBALLED.

THE
GALLEY
(cont'd) ☐

7.19   GAS COOKING:

☐ - GAS BOTTLES ARE STOWED ON DECK OR
IN A GAS-TIGHT LOCKER WITH A DRAIN
OVERBOARD ABOVE THE WATERLINE.

☐ - A VALVE IS SITED NEAR THE STOVE IN
ORDER THAT THE GAS CAN BE - AND IS -
TURNED OFF WHENEVER THE STOVE IS NOT
IN USE. Have a notice about this,
which is in addition to turning off
at the bottle when leaving the boat.

☐ - PIPING BETWEEN BOTTLES AND STOVE
MUST BE BEST SEAMLESS COPPER,
FITTED PROFESSIONALLY.

☐ 7.20   ON ANY GIMBALLED STOVE (GAS OR
OTHERWISE) THE FLEXIBLE TUBING LEADING TO
THE STOVE MUST BE ARMOURED, FIRE-PROOF
QUALITY - NOT RUBBER OR PLASTIC.

☐ 7.21   WITH AN ALCOHOL STOVE, OR ANY OTHER
TYPE OF LIQUID FUEL STOVE HAVING A
PRESSURE TANK, THE CUT-OFF VALVE FOR THE
FUEL IS SITED AT THE FRONT OR SIDE OF THE
STOVE, NOT AT THE REAR. With a flare-up,
it might be impossible to reach the back
of the stove.

SECTION 8   ORGANISATION

SECURITY ☐   8.1 ALL DOORS AND HATCHES HAVE SECURE

LOCKS. Keys hidden in most of the

traditional places such as ventilators or

deck lockers can usually be easily found.

☐   8.2 DESPITE A LOCKED BOAT, A FURTHER

SECURE STOWAGE IS AVAILABLE FOR

BINOCULARS, RADIOS, WATCHES, ETC.

☐   8.3 AN INVENTORY HAS BEEN MADE OF THE

CONTENTS OF THE YACHT. This should

include the serial number of outboard

motors, binoculars, and any other valuable

item that has a serial number (p.126).

☐   8.4 A COPY OF THIS INVENTORY IS KEPT

ASHORE. This may be needed for any

insurance claim.

COAST- ☐   8.5 IN THE UK COMPLETE AND **RETURN** THE
GUARD YACHT
& BOAT   SPECIAL FORM CG 66 (AVAILABLE FROM
SAFETY
SCHEME   COASTGUARD OR HARBOUR MASTER) GIVING

DETAILS OF THE BOAT, EQUIPMENT AND

NORMAL CRUISING AREA. In any event ensure

that somebody reliable knows your

intentions, and don't forget to advise

your safe arrival at your destination or

at any alternative port of call.

SHIP'S
PAPERS
ETC.

8.6 SHIP'S PAPERS ARE AVAILABLE IN SECURE STOWAGE ONBOARD (not lost in a drawer).

- [ ] - REGISTRATION CERTIFICATE, OR INTERNATIONAL CERTIFICATE FOR PLEASURE NAVIGATION
- [ ] - LICENCE FOR RADIO TRANSMITTER (SHIP LICENCE)
- [ ] - RADIO OPERATOR'S LICENCE
- [ ] - BILL OF SALE
- [ ] - BUILDER'S CERTIFICATE
- [ ] - LOCAL WATERWAYS LICENCE (WHERE RELEVANT)
- [ ] - MOD WARRANT FOR SPECIAL ENSIGN (U.K.)

[ ] 8.7 PHOTOCOPIES KEPT ASHORE OF IMPORTANT PAPERS KEPT ONBOARD.

[ ] 8.8 SHIP'S DRAWINGS ARE ONBOARD AND AVAILABLE FOR REFERENCE. All boats, other than very small ones, will have been provided with certain drawings by the builder - if only a hull plan and a wiring diagram.

SHIP'S
PAPERS ETC.
(cont'd)

☐ 8.9 SHIP'S DRAWINGS HAVE BEEN UP-DATED
WHEN ALTERATIONS HAVE BEEN CARRIED OUT.
This especially applies to wiring diagrams
after additional equipment has been
fitted.

☐ 8.10 MANUALS FOR THE VARIOUS ITEMS OF
EQUIPMENT ONBOARD ARE KEPT AVAILABLE FOR
REFERENCE. Just about every item of
equipment onboard will have been supplied
with some sort of operating and
maintenance instructions by the
manufacturers. These will vary from a
sizeable handbook for the engine down to a
single piece of paper for the pressure
cooker. They are all important and must
be kept, preferably in a folder.

BOAT'S
NAME

☐ 8.11 THE BOAT'S NAME IS PROMINENTLY
DISPLAYED ON EITHER SIDE IN ADDITION TO
ACROSS THE STERN. This is not a legal
requirement, but it is good sense to make
the boat easy to identify, both in port
and at sea. Sailing boats may have their
names displayed in 12 in (300 mm) letters
on weather cloths either side of their
cockpits. Power cruisers will normally
have name boards either side of their
steering position.

Section 8

MAINTEN-
ANCE
RECORDS

8.12 A SIMPLE RECORD IS KEPT OF ALL THE
REPAIR AND MAJOR MAINTENANCE WORK DONE
ONBOARD. This should include boatyard
work, jobs done by visiting workmen and
major items done by the owner or his crew.
Bills should be kept. This helps keep
track of expenditure and makes future
budgeting easier. Maintenance is better
planned when it is known what has been
done before, and when. It is also helpful
for any technician to know what previous
work has been done onboard.

SECTION 9   TOOLS, MAINTENANCE GEAR, AND SPARES

TOOL KITS   9.1 A proper tool kit with handy stowage
is essential in any boat and a suggested
minimum is listed in 9.2

9.2 BASIC ESSENTIAL TOOL KIT

- [ ] SPANNERS/WRENCHES ¼ in - 1 in + METRIC
- [ ] ADJUSTABLE SPANNERS/WRENCHES - 2 sizes
- [ ] MOLE OR VICE GRIPS
- [ ] SLIP JOINT PLIERS
- [ ] SCREWDRIVERS - 3 sizes
- [ ] 'PHILLIPS' SCREWDRIVER
- [ ] STUB SCREWDRIVER
- [ ] MIDGET SCREWDRIVER (for electrical work)
- [ ] ELECTRICAL PLIERS
- [ ] NEEDLENOSE PLIERS
- [ ] HAMMER
- [ ] COLD CHISEL
- [ ] PUNCH
- [ ] KNIFE
- [ ] HACKSAW & BLADES
- [ ] HAND DRILL AND DRILL SET
- [ ] FILES - ROUND AND FLAT
- [ ] 'ALLEN' KEYS - SET

Section 9

9.3 Lists of maintenance gear, recommended for any boat follow in section 9.4 - 9.7. They include such things as adhesives, tape and other items needed both for day-to-day maintenance and emergency repairs. A surprising variety of repairs can be achieved with epoxy glue! These lists are reasonably comprehensive, but all the items will be found useful sooner or later.

9.4 MAINTENANCE GEAR - GENERAL

- [ ] LIGHT OIL (eg 3 in 1)
- [ ] ANTI-CORROSIVE SPRAY (WD40)
- [ ] ALL PURPOSE GREASE
- [ ] GREASE GUN
- [ ] SILICONE SPRAY
- [ ] SILICONE CAULKING COMPOUND
- [ ] PLASTIC TAPE - VARIOUS COLOURS (PTFE)
- [ ] ADHESIVE - GENERAL PURPOSE
- [ ] EPOXY GLUE (Araldite)
- [ ] FASTENINGS - Nuts, bolts, washers, screws, copper nails, etc, a good selection, stowed in a compartmented plastic box.

MAINTENANCE
GEAR
(cont'd)

9.5 ELECTRICAL

☐ ELECTRICAL TAPE   ☐ JUMPER CABLES

☐ TEST METER OR LAMP   ☐ DISTILLED WATER

☐ BATTERY FILLER   ☐ CABLE CONNECTORS

☐ HYDROMETER   ☐ SCREWDRIVER

9.6 MECHANICAL

☐ WATER PUMP GREASE

☐ STERN TUBE PACKING (Check size is correct)

☐ PACKING FOR RUDDER POST GLAND (if fitted)

☐ NYLON JOINTING TAPE

☐ LIQUID GASKET MATERIAL (Permatex)

☐ GASKET MATERIAL

☐ PLASTIC TUBING - various sizes

☐ HOSE CLIPS - various sizes

9.7 DECK

☐ KNIFE   ☐ LASHING CORD

☐ MARLINE SPIKE   ☐ WHIPPING TWINE

☐ PLIERS   ☐ MARLINE

☐ SHACKLER   ☐ SHOCK CORD

☐ SPLIT PINS   ☐ SPARE FLAG HALYARD

SPARE GEAR   9.8 Unless they are cruising in areas
where spare parts cannot be obtained,
most boats can restrict their outfit of
spares to those items that might be needed
for emergency repairs at sea. Lists of
essential spares are shown in 9.12 - 9.14.

☐   9.9 A LIST IS KEPT OF SPARES ONBOARD,
AND WHERE THEY ARE STOWED. This should
apply even when only a modest outfit of
spares is carried. Spares, when needed,
are often required in a hurry, and it
must be possible to find them quickly.

☐   9.10 A RECORD IS KEPT WHEN SPARES ARE
USED - SO THAT REPLACEMENTS ARE OBTAINED.

☐   9.11 SPARES ARE MARKED SHOWING WHERE
THEY SHOULD BE USED. Many items (belts,
fuses, bulbs, hoses, etc) look alike.
They should be marked as soon as they are
brought onboard and before being stowed.
Replaced items which can be kept as
emergency spares should be clearly marked,
those for repair should be landed and
all others thrown away.

SPARE
GEAR
(cont'd)

9.12 ENGINE & GENERATOR SPARES

General

☐ IMPELLERS FOR WATER PUMPS

☐ DRIVE BELTS FOR ALTERNATORS ETC - one of
each type

☐ FILTER ELEMENTS FOR FUEL FILTERS

☐ LUBRICATING OIL FILTER

☐ HOSES

Diesel Engines

☐ SPARE INJECTORS

☐ AT LEAST ONE HIGH PRESSURE FUEL PIPE
(LONGEST SIZE)

☐ GASKET SET

Note: These items are important, but need
not be essential if spares are easily
obtainable in normal cruising area.

Petrol Engines

☐ SPARK PLUGS

☐ POINTS

☐ COIL

Outboard Engines

☐ SPARK PLUGS

☐ PROPELLER

☐ SHEAR PINS & SPLIT PINS (WHERE NEEDED)

SPARE
GEAR
(cont'd)

9.13 ELECTRICAL SPARES

☐ FLASHLIGHT BATTERIES AND BULBS

☐ BATTERIES FOR RADIO AND OTHER ELECTRONIC
GEAR

☐ BULBS (INCLUDING COMPASS, NAVIGATION
LIGHTS, INSTRUMENT LIGHTS, ETC)

☐ FUSES (CHECK EQUIPMENT THAT HAS FUSES,
AND HAVE EXACT SPARES)

9.14 GENERAL SPARES

☐ IMPELLERS FOR ANY PUMPS (TOILETS, BILGE
PUMPS ETC) WHICH USE RUBBER OR NEOPRENE
IMPELLERS

☐ DIAPHRAGMS FOR BILGE PUMPS (WHERE NEEDED)

☐ COMPLETE SPARES KIT FOR TOILET

☐ SAILMAKING AND RIGGING (See 10.19, 10.20)

SECTION 10   SAILS AND RIGGING CHECK

RIGGING ☐   10.1 STANDING RIGGING IS SET UP AS
NECESSARY, AND ALL RIGGING SCREWS OR
TURNBUCKLES ARE SECURED WITH EITHER SCREWS
OR SPLIT PINS. EXPOSED SPLIT PINS ARE
TAPED TO PREVENT SNAGGING. TOGGLES SHOULD
BE FITTED TO STANDING RIGGING TO PREVENT
FATIGUE FAILURE. The tensions on shrouds
and stays must be as correct for cruising
as for racing. If in doubt, get help.

☐   10.2 THE INBOARD ENDS OF HALYARDS ARE
EITHER SECURED OR TIED WITH STOPPER KNOTS
SO THAT THEY CAN NEVER ESCAPE ALOFT.

ALOFT   10.3 SOMEONE GOES UP FOR REGULAR
INSPECTION ALOFT.

☐   - RIGGING SCREWS OR TURNBUCKLES AND
SHACKLES ARE SECURED AND TAPED.

☐   -- THERE ARE NO FATIGUE CRACKS ON
MASTHEAD CRANE OR SHROUD TANGS.

☐   - SPREADERS ARE SECURE AT INBOARD
END.

☐   - OUTBOARD ENDS OF SPREADERS HAVE
ANTI-CHAFE GEAR WHERE NECESSARY TO
AVOID CHAFING HEADSAILS.

REEFING   10.4 PHYSICAL CHECK AS FOLLOWS:

☐   - ROLLER REEFING IS LUBRICATED AS
           NECESSARY AND WORKS FREELY.

☐   - REEFING HANDLE HAS A SPECIAL HANDY
           STOWAGE, AND THERE IS A SPARE.

☐   - SLAB OR JIFFY REEFING - REEF
           CORDAGE IS STOWED IN A MARKED BAG
           AND NOT USED FOR ANY OTHER PURPOSE.

SAILS   ☐ 10.5 SAILS ARE MARKED WITH THEIR NAME OR
           NUMBER. SAIL BAGS SHOULD BE MARKED WITH
           SAIL AND BOAT'S NAME.

☐ 10.6 SAIL BAGS ARE CLEARLY MARKED WITH
           THEIR CONTENTS, PREFERABLY IN SEVERAL
           PLACES. This makes them easy to spot.

☐ 10.7 HEADSAIL HANKS OILED AND FREE.

☐ 10.8 TACKS OF SAILS ARE MARKED.

STORM   ☐ 10.9 STORM SAILS ARE SET AT LEAST ONCE
SAILS   EACH SEASON. Many boats go for long
           periods without setting their storm
           sails. And the one time they are needed
           is no occasion to find that the hanks are
           too stiff or that the sheets are wrong.

GENERAL
MAINTENANCE

☐ 10.10 WINCHES MAINTAINED AND FREE RUNNING

☐ 10.11 FASTENINGS SECURING WINCHES ARE
CHECKED - PARTICULARLY IMPORTANT FOR
HALYARD WINCHES ON WOODEN MASTS.

☐ 10.12 RIGGING SCREWS OR TURNBUCKLES
ARE GREASED, AND LOCKED.

☐ 10.13 SNAP SHACKLES ON HALYARDS AND TACK
FITTINGS ARE LUBRICATED. They are easier
to work if the piston is fitted with a
short lanyard (no loops, which can get
snagged).

☐ 10.14 SPINNAKER POLE FITTINGS LUBRICATED.

☐ 10.15 WIRE TO ROPE SPLICES ON HALYARDS
ARE SOUND AND FREE FROM BARBS.

☐ 10.16 SAIL COVERS ARE A NEAT FIT,
LASHINGS ARE STRONG AND TIDY, WITH NO
LOOSE OR FRAYED ENDS.

☐ 10.17 THE FALLS OF HALYARDS ARE NEATLY
COILED AND SECURED.

☐ SAIL TIES   ☐ SAIL COVER(S)

☐ SAIL BATTENS   ☐ BOOM CRUTCH or SLING

☐ BOOM VANG STROP   ☐ KICKING STRAP (VANG

☐ REEFING HANDLE   TACKLE)

   + SPARE   ☐ REEF PENDANTS/

☐ WINCH HANDLES   LASHINGS

☐ HEADSAIL SHEET   ☐ SPINNAKER SHEET

   BLOCKS   BLOCKS

☐ SHEETS: MAIN   ☐ SPINNAKER SHEETS

          MIZZEN   ☐ SPINNAKER GUYS

          HEAD-   ☐ BOSUN'S CHAIR
          SAILS

10.19   SAILMAKER'S BAG

☐ NEEDLES   ☐ SPARE CLOTH

☐ PALM   ☐ REPAIR TAPE

☐ WAXED THREAD   ☐ SPARE HANKS & SLIDES

☐ SPIKE   ☐ KNIFE OR SCISSORS

10.20   RIGGER'S BAG

☐ CABLE CLAMPS   ☐ SEIZING WIRE

☐ SPARE SHACKLES   ☐ ANTI-CHAFE TAPE

☐ SPLIT PINS   ☐ SPARE TOGGLES

☐ SPLICING TOOL   ☐ HEAT SHRINK SLEEVES

PART II

On deck, worn varnish or a loose whipping on a halyard act as visual reminders that something needs to be done. But a corroded hose clip on a water pipe may go unnoticed unless someone is specifically looking for it. Which is why there is a need for regular checks onboard - rather than a haphazard 'look around'.

Nothing in a boat can be taken for granted. Because the bilge pump, the radio, or the navigation lights were working last weekend, it does not mean that they do not need checking now. The results of an equipment failure are likely to be far more serious in an aircraft than in a boat, but the meticulous way in which an airline pilot checks his plane does have some relevance for the boat owner.

The check lists in this section are designed so that the various parts of the boat and her equipment are inspected and checked as often as is reasonably necessary without spending a disproportionate amount of time.

SECTION 11   <u>FITTING OUT CHECK</u>

During fitting out it is desirable, if
time permits, to carry out all the
appropriate checks in Part I of this
manual - although certain items are
repeated here.

All machinery and equipment should be
tested before leaving the berth or mooring,
and then a short sea trial carried out.
This gives a chance to make good any
defects, or to collect items overlooked
before starting the first cruise or
passage.

The following may vary in detail according
to how the yacht has been laid up.

HULL   ☐   SEACOCKS - VALVES WORK FREELY, APPEAR
SOUND AND FREE FROM CORROSION, PIPES ARE
SECURELY ATTACHED.

       ☐   BILGES - CLEAN AND FREE FROM DEBRIS.
LIMBER HOLES CLEAR. It is important to
check this after any work onboard, when
wood shavings or other rubbish may have
fallen into the bilge.

HULL
(cont'd)

☐ BILGE PUMPS - MANUAL AND ELECTRICAL/
MECHANICAL - ACTUALLY TESTED. Ultimately
the only effective test of a bilge pump
is that it does pump water out of the
bilge and over the side; water should be
put into the bilges in order to give the
pumps a proper test. Leaking or blocked
suction and discharge lines can prevent
the system from working, even though the
pump itself may be functioning.

☐ STEERING IS TESTED. With wheel steering:
LEAD OF STEERING CABLES IS INSPECTED,
SHEAVES ARE SECURE AND WORKING FREELY,
CABLES ARE FIRMLY SECURED TO RUDDER HEAD.
Tiller: NO PLAY, SPLITS OR CRACKS.

☐ GEAR IS STOWED CLEAR OF QUADRANT OR
RUDDER HEAD, AND RUDDER POST BEARING IS
INSPECTED FOR LEAKS.

☐ FRESH WATER TANKS FILLED. PUMPS TESTED
AND SYSTEM CHECKED FOR LEAKS.

☐ TOILETS TESTED AND FREE FROM LEAKS.

☐ HATCHES, PORTS, AND WINDOWS HOSE TESTED
FOR LEAKS.

Section 11

ENGINE(S) ☐   ENGINE PREPARED FOR OPERATION IF IT HAS
AND   BEEN 'WINTERISED'.
GENERATORS

☐   ENGINE OIL, OIL FILTER, AND FUEL FILTERS
CHANGED (if this has not been done during
or before lay up).

☐   DRIVE BELTS INSPECTED FOR SOUNDNESS AND
CORRECT TENSION. They should deflect
about ½ in (12 mm) under pressure from
one finger.

☐   ENGINE COOLING WATER INTAKE - SEACOCK IS
WORKING FREELY AND STRAINER IS CLEAN.

☐   COOLING WATER HOSES ARE SOUND, HOSE CLIPS
ARE TIGHT. NO LEAKS.

☐   ENGINE STARTING BATTERIES CHARGED AND
CONNECTED. TERMINALS CLEAN. ELECTROLYTE
LEVEL CORRECT.

☐   ENGINE RUN AT IDLE AND THEN RUN IN GEAR
ALONGSIDE BEFORE SEA TRIAL.
- COOLING WATER CIRCULATING
- OIL PRESSURE NORMAL
- AMMETER SHOWS ALTERNATOR IS CHARGING
- THROTTLE AND GEAR CONTROL WORKING FREELY

Section 11

ENGINE(S) ☐   TOOL KITS AND ESSENTIAL SPARES CHECKED.
AND
GENERATORS   (Section 9).
(cont'd)

GENERATORS   AS FOR ENGINE.

☐   TEST UNDER LOAD.

ELECTRICS ☐   SERVICE BATTERIES AND BATTERY TERMINALS
CHECKED.

☐   NAVIGATION LIGHTS, COMPASS LIGHT,
INSTRUMENT LIGHTS, AND ANCHOR LIGHT
TESTED.

DECK   ☐   INSPECT MOORING LINES AND FENDERS.

☐   ANCHOR WINDLASS - BRAKES AND CLUTCH ARE
FREE, AND ANCHOR CAN BE LET GO.

☐   LET GO SHORT LENGTH OF ANCHOR CHAIN/LINE
AND TEST WINDLASS UNDER LOAD.

☐   DINGHIES - INFLATABLE AND OTHERWISE -
CHECK EQUIPMENT (see 1.29 - 1.39).

☐   INFLATABLE DINGHIES - INFLATE AND CHECK
FOR LEAKS.

☐   DE-WINTERISE OUTBOARD MOTOR AND TEST.

Section 11

SAFETY ☐ <u>CARRY OUT COMPLETE SAFETY EQUIPMENT CHECK</u> (Sections 14 and 15).

NAVIGA-
TION ☐ CHECK COMPASS.

☐ TEST INSTRUMENTS - DEPTH SOUNDER, LOG, ETC.

☐ CHECK PROTRACTOR, PENCILS, DIVIDERS, ETC.

☐ CHECK CHARTS ARE COMPLETE AND UP-TO-DATE.

☐ PUT ONBOARD NEW EDITIONS OF ALMANACS, TIDE TABLES, ETC. DISPOSE OF OLD EDITIONS, AND DO NOT KEEP ONBOARD.

GALLEY
AND
DOMESTIC ☐ FILL UP STOVE FUEL. CHECK STOVE OPERATION. CHECK SYSTEM FOR LEAKS.

GENERAL ☐ CHECK INSURANCE COVERS NEW PERIOD AFLOAT AND START OF ACTIVE CRUISING.

☐ CHECK ALL ITEMS WHICH WERE LANDED FOR REPAIR, STORE, ETC, ARE BACK ONBOARD.

☐ CHECK SHIP'S PAPERS ONBOARD.

Section 11

SAILS ☐ CHECK ALL SAILS ARE ONBOARD.

☐ RIGGING SET UP AND RIGGING SCREWS OR
TURNBUCKLES MOUSED.

☐ INSPECTION ALOFT IF MAST HAS NOT BEEN
UNSTEPPED (See 10.3).

☐ HALYARDS RE-ROVE, SHACKLES OILED, LOWER
ENDS OF HALYARDS SECURE TO PREVENT GOING
ALOFT.

☐ MAIN SHEET RE-ROVE, HEADSAIL SHEETS
CHECKED AND STOWED.

☐ WINCHES INSPECTED AND SERVICED IF
NECESSARY.

☐ SHEET LEAD BLOCKS SITED AND STOWED.

☐ BATTENS ON BOARD.

☐ WINCH HANDLES ABOARD.

SECTION 12   HAUL OUT CHECK

Notes: Whether a boat is hauled out only
for painting, or whether she is laid up
ashore, it is important to take the
opportunity to do those jobs that can
only be done while the boat is dried out.

Not all brands of anti-fouling paint will
'take' on each other. It is best to stick
to the same brand and type, but if a
change is necessary, check with your yard
or chandler, or the maker, that the new
paint is compatible.

☐ INSPECT ALL SEACOCKS AND TEST THE VALVES.

☐ INSPECT ANTI-ELECTROLYSIS SACRIFICIAL
ZINC ANODES. RENEW ANY THAT ARE BADLY
WASTED. CHECK ELECTRICAL EARTHING GOOD.

☐ INSPECT ALL WATER INTAKES (ENGINE COOLING,
TOILETS, ETC.). REMOVE AND CLEAN
STRAINERS.

☐ ECHO SOUNDER. THE TRANSDUCER IN THE HULL
SHOULD BE CLEANED OFF BUT (NORMALLY) NOT
PAINTED WITH ANTI-FOULING; DO NOT SCRAPE.

☐ LOGS/SPEEDOMETERS. ANY RETRACTABLE
FITTINGS SHOULD BE WITHDRAWN. TAKE CARE
THAT ANY OTHERS ARE NOT DAMAGED DURING
HAUL OUT. NORMALLY THESE FITTINGS SHOULD
NOT BE PAINTED WITH ANTI-FOULING PAINT,
BUT CHECK INSTRUCTION MANUAL.

☐ INSPECT RUDDER FITTINGS CAREFULLY. IF IN
DOUBT ABOUT THEIR SOUNDNESS, GET EXPERT
ADVICE. CHECK FOR EXCESSIVE PLAY.

☐ INSPECT STERN GLAND AND SHAFT BEARINGS
FOR WEAR. IF STERN GLAND HAS BEEN LEAKING
AND RE-PACKING IS DESIRABLE, THIS IS THE
TIME TO DO IT. IF NECESSARY GET EXPERT
ADVICE.

☐ REMOVE ANCHOR CHAIN FROM LOCKER AND FLAKE
OUT ASHORE. INSPECT FOR EXCESSIVE WEAR
OR CORROSION. RENEW MARKINGS. CLEAN
OUT CABLE LOCKER AND CHECK DRAINAGE.

☐ CHECK PROPELLER(S).

☐ COMPLETE OWN BOAT DATA ON PAGE 123.

SECTION 13   PRE-SAILING CHECK

- [ ] FUEL
- [ ] FRESH WATER
- [ ] SPARE LUBRICATING OIL
  (for engine & gearbox)
- [ ] COOKING GAS/STOVE FUEL
- [ ] OUTBOARD FUEL & OIL
- [ ] STERN TUBE LUBRICATION

ENGINE(S) AND GENERATOR:
- [ ] OIL LEVEL
- [ ] FRESH COOLING WATER
- [ ] GEARBOX & THROTTLE CONTROLS TESTED

- [ ] STEERING TESTED
- [ ] BATTERIES - ELECTROLYTE
              - SWITCHED ON
- [ ] BILGES DRY
- [ ] INSTRUMENTS AND RADIO TESTED
- [ ] COMPASS & NAVIGATION LIGHTS TESTED
- [ ] HATCHES & PORTHOLES FASTENED
- [ ] BELOW DECKS SECURED FOR SEA, INCLUDING
  GALLEY
- [ ] ANCHOR READY FOR LETTING GO
- [ ] ENSIGN AND BURGEE HOISTED

Section 13

☐ WEATHER FORECAST OBTAINED

☐ BAROMETER READING NOTED

☐ TIME OF HW/LW. DIRECTION OF TIDAL STREAM

☐ COURSE ON LEAVING HARBOUR

☐ PORT/HARBOUR ENTRY OR DEPARTURE SIGNALS

☐ LOG READING AND ENGINE HOURS RECORDED

☐ UNLESS CRUISING LOCALLY, COASTGUARD OR
OTHER AUTHORITY INFORMED OF INTENTIONS
(SAFE ARRIVAL MUST ALSO BE REPORTED)

After starting engine:

☐ ENGINE COOLING WATER CIRCULATING

☐ ENGINE OIL PRESSURE NORMAL

☐ AMMETER SHOWS BATTERIES BEING CHARGED

After underway:

☐ FENDERS INBOARD AND STOWED

☐ ALL OTHER DECK GEAR STOWED

☐ ANCHOR SECURED (after clear of narrow
waters)

SECTION 14   SAFETY EQUIPMENT CHECK

For full details of safety equipment onboard see section 3, and Own Boat Data on page 119.

EACH ITEM OF EQUIPMENT TO BE :

☐ SIGHTED

☐ FOUND IN CORRECT STOWAGE

☐ TESTED (where starred *)

☐ LIFERAFT   ☐ EMERGENCY RATIONS

☐ LIFEJACKETS   ☐ EMERGENCY WATER

☐ SAFETY HARNESSES   ☐ RADAR REFLECTOR
  *(check clips)   (catch-rain mode)

☐ MEDICAL KIT   ☐ *HORN

☐ *FLASHLIGHTS   ☐ *BUOYANT LIGHTS

☐ SPECIAL TOOLS   ☐ MAN OVERBOARD GEAR
  (wire cutters)   *(clear to throw)

☐ LEAKSTOPPERS   ☐ FIRE EXTINGUISHERS
  (wooden plugs)   *(easy to unclip)

☐ FLARES   ☐ DISTRESS RADIO
  *(accessible)   *(battery condition)

Dates due for servicing:

LIFERAFT   . . . .

LIFEJACKETS - Oral inflation. . . . .

                CO_2 inflation. . . . .

FIRE EXTINGUISHERS   . . . .
(including fixed installation
in engine compartment)

FLARES -   Expiry date. . . . .

SECTION 15   CREW SAFETY CHECK

THE CREW MUST KNOW THE STOWAGE OF ALL
ITEMS OF SAFETY EQUIPMENT, AS IN SECTION
14 AND OWN BOAT DATA ON PAGE 119.
This is particularly important in respect
of items which are not normally visible
such as lifejackets, harnesses, flares,
medical kit, tools and flashlights.

CREW MUST KNOW:-

☐ WHERE LIFEJACKETS ARE STOWED AND HOW TO
USE THEM.

☐ WHERE HARNESSES ARE STOWED, WHEN AND HOW
TO USE THEM.

☐ HOW TO LAUNCH THE LIFERAFT.

☐ HOW TO USE THE FIRE EXTINGUISHERS (WITHOUT
STOPPING TO READ THE INSTRUCTIONS).

☐ HOW TO DEAL WITH A 'MAN OVERBOARD'
SITUATION, INCLUDING HOW TO RECOVER HIM
ONBOARD.

☐ THE CORRECT USE OF FLARES IN AN EMERGENCY,
AND HOW TO OPERATE THEM - EVEN IN THE
DARK.

☐ SOMEONE - IN ADDITION TO THE SKIPPER -
SHOULD KNOW ELEMENTARY FIRST AID,
INCLUDING MOUTH TO MOUTH RESUSCITATION.

☐ SOMEONE AS WELL AS THE SKIPPER SHOULD KNOW
HOW TO MAKE A DISTRESS CALL ON THE RADIO
TELEPHONE (See 3.25)

SECTION 16   GOING ASHORE CHECK

ALONG-
SIDE
☐ CHECK SUFFICIENT FENDERS OUT. It is wise to put fenders on the outboard side for the possible arrival of another boat.

☐ CHECK MOORING LINES WELL SECURED, DOUBLED UP IF NECESSARY, AND PROPERLY ADJUSTED. If lying outside another boat or boats, take your own lines out to shore fore and aft.

☐ IF RISE AND FALL OF TIDE IS APPRECIABLE, CHECK SUFFICIENT SCOPE IN MOORING LINES.

☐ PLACE CHAFE GEAR IN FAIRLEADS.

ON A
MOORING
OR AT
ANCHOR
☐ MOORING CHAIN OR PENDANT WELL SECURED.

☐ TRIPPING LINE ON ANCHOR (IF APPROPRIATE).

☐ CHAFING GEAR IN BOW FAIRLEAD.

☐ SWITCH ON ANCHOR LIGHT OR HOIST BLACK BALL IN RIGGING (IF APPROPRIATE).

☐ CHECK ANCHOR BEARINGS WHERE APPROPRIATE, TO BE CLEAR OF ALL OBSTRUCTIONS WHEN TIDE TURNS OR IF WIND CHANGES.

Section 16

GENERAL ☐ CHECK DEPTH BELOW KEEL AGAINST TIDAL STATE
TO ENSURE BOAT WILL NOT GROUND.

☐ SEACOCKS CLOSED - ENGINE INTAKE, SINK
OUTLET, TOILET ETC.

☐ COOKING GAS TURNED OFF AT ALL APPLIANCES,
AND AT GAS BOTTLE.

☐ HATCHES AND PORTS CLOSED AND SECURE.

☐ LIFERAFT TAKEN BELOW AND ALL OTHER
ATTRACTIVE AND PORTABLE ITEMS STOWED
SECURELY.

☐ OUTBOARD REMOVED FROM DINGHY INTO LOCKED
STOWAGE.

☐ ALL ELECTRIC AND ELECTRONIC EQUIPMENT
(RADIO, ECHO SOUNDER, LOG, WIND
INSTRUMENTS ETC) SWITCHED OFF. BATTERY
ISOLATED.

☐ PERISHABLES REMOVED FROM GALLEY.

Section 16

GENERAL
(cont'd)

☐ ALL RUBBISH TAKEN ASHORE.

☐ ICE BOX/REFRIGERATOR OPEN IF NOT IN USE.

☐ DIRTY LAUNDRY DEALT WITH.

☐ DEFECT LIST, YARD WORK LIST, SHOPPING
LIST, ETC MADE OUT AND TAKEN ASHORE IF
NEEDED.

☐ MONEY/CHEQUE BOOK/CREDIT CARD/PASSPORT
TAKEN ASHORE; CAR KEYS.

☐ VALUABLE ITEMS LOCKED UP - EVEN IF BOAT
IS LOCKED.

☐ AUTOMATIC BILGE PUMP (IF FITTED) TO
'AUTO'.

☐ GAS, BILGE, BURGLAR ALARMS (IF FITTED)
SWITCHED ON.

☐ MAIN ELECTRICS SWITCHED OFF.

Section 16

SAILS & RIGGING

☐ HALYARDS SECURED CLEAR OF THE MAST.

☐ BOOM CRUTCH RIGGED, MAIN SHEET SECURED.

☐ MAINSAIL CLEW EASED.

☐ SAIL COVERS ON AND LASHED.

☐ SAILS BAGGED AND STOWED.

☐ SAILS TAKEN ASHORE FOR WASHING OR SAILMAKER AS REQUIRED.

☐ SHEETS, BLOCKS, WINCH HANDLES, ETC STOWED BELOW.

☐ TILLER OR WHEEL LASHED.

☐ ADJUSTABLE STAYS EASED AS REQUIRED.

☐ BOOM VANG/KICKING STRAP RELEASED.

☐ FLAGS HAULED DOWN.

SECTION 17   PRE-CRUISE CHECK

The annual programme for many boats is to cruise locally for most of the season, and to undertake the occasional longer trip, possibly for the owner's annual holiday.

HULL   ☐ ALL SEACOCKS SIGHTED AND IN GOOD ORDER; VALVES TESTED AND WORKING FREELY.

☐ BILGE PUMPS TESTED.

☐ STERN TUBES INSPECTED FOR LEAKS AND ADJUSTED IF NECESSARY. STERN TUBE LUBRICATION SATISFACTORY.

☐ RUDDER POST BEARING INSPECTED FOR LEAKS.

ENGINE(S) ☐ ALL ENGINE MAINTENANCE DONE (see 4.18).

ENGINE(S) & GENERATOR:
☐ - BELTS TIGHT AND FREE FROM WEAR.

☐ - NO COOLING WATER OR LUBRICATING OIL LEAKS VISIBLE.

☐ - HOSES AND HOSE CLIPS SOUND.

☐ - STRAINER ON COOLING WATER INTAKE CLEAN, VALVE FREE.

Section 17

RADIO & ☐ ALL RADIO AND ELECTRONIC EQUIPMENT TESTED
GENERATORS AND FOUND OPERATIONAL.

GALLEY ☐ GALLEY STOVE - GAS PIPING INSPECTED AND
FREE FROM LEAKS.

SAILS ☐ WINCHES WORKING FREELY.
ETC.

☐ ROUTINE INSPECTION ALOFT CARRIED OUT (See
10.3).

☐ HALYARDS SECURED BELOW AND IN SOUND
CONDITION (See 10.2).

☐ ALL SAILS INSPECTED FOR CHAFE.

☐ SLIDES AND BATTENS ON MAINSAIL AND MIZZEN
SOUND. SPARES ONBOARD.

☐ STORM SAILS ONBOARD.

☐ REEFING ARRANGEMENTS CHECKED. REEFING
GEAR SIGHTED (LASHINGS, PENDANTS, ETC. OR
HANDLE AND SPARE) (See 10.4).

☐ ALL SHEETS INSPECTED FOR WEAR AND ENDS
NOT FRAYED.

☐ SHACKLES TESTED FOR TIGHTNESS/SECURITY.

Section 17

NAVIGATIONAL
PLANNING

In motor boats it is important to plan passages or cruises with due regard to fuel consumption. This also applies to sailing boats, which may wish to use the engine for several hours on end in order to maintain a schedule.

☐ WORK OUT IN ADVANCE THE DISTANCES AND COMPASS COURSES (KEEPING WELL CLEAR OF ALL DANGERS) ALONG THE INTENDED ROUTE.

☐ WORK OUT THE TIDAL HEIGHTS AND THE GENERAL DIRECTIONS OF TIDAL STREAMS FOR HARBOURS AND AREA CONCERNED. YOU SHOULD BE AWARE OF WHETHER IT IS SPRINGS OR NEAPS, AND THE IMPLICATIONS FOR THE AREA UNDER CONSIDERATION.

☐ CHECK ON RECENT NOTICES TO MARINERS AND OTHER LOCAL NAVIGATIONAL WARNINGS COVERING THE AREA TO BE VISITED.

☐ CHECK NECESSARY CHARTS, SAILING DIRECTIONS, PILOT GUIDES ETC. ONBOARD AND UP TO DATE. Charts should be carried not only for harbours on the itinerary, but also for those which might have to be visited as a bad weather diversion.

NAVIGA-
TIONAL
PLANNING
(cont'd)

☐ LIST PORTS/HARBOURS/ANCHORAGES LIKELY TO
BE VISITED. INVESTIGATE NAVIGATIONAL
DETAILS (INCLUDING PRINCIPAL LIGHTS/
BEACONS ETC., LEADING MARKS, ENTRY
SIGNALS), MOORINGS AND ANCHORAGES,
LANDING PLACES, FACILITIES. The list
should also include places of refuge in
the event of bad weather.

☐ FIND OUT WHERE/HOW TO GET SHIPPING/
WEATHER FORECASTS FOR INTENDED CRUISING
AREA. CHECK ON RADIO FREQUENCIES.

☐ IF SEXTANT NAVIGATION IS USED, CHECK
CHRONOMETER/DECK WATCH ERROR AND RATE.

☐ CHECK PROVISIONS, GALLEY FUEL.

☐ IF NECESSARY WARN CREW IN ADVANCE ABOUT
BRINGING RIGHT GEAR - FOUL WEATHER/WARM
CLOTHING, RIG FOR SHORE FUNCTIONS ETC.

GOING
FOREIGN

☐ CERTIFICATE OF REGISTRY MUST BE ONBOARD.
If boat not registered, obtain
International Certificate for Pleasure
Navigation, or other ship's papers.

☐ ENSURE VALID PASSPORTS HELD AND ONBOARD
FOR ALL CREW.

Section 17

GOING
FOREIGN
(cont'd)

☐ SHOULD ANY CREW BE OF ANOTHER NATIONALITY, IT IS ESSENTIAL TO CLEAR WITH IMMIGRATION.

☐ INFORM LOCAL CUSTOMS OF YOUR DEPARTURE FOR ABROAD, FILLING IN THE RELEVANT FORM WHICH WILL BE SUPPLIED.

☐ IF BOAT IS CHARTERED, MAKE CERTAIN INSURERS ARE INFORMED AND COVER IS PROVIDED. Charter Agreement must also be carried aboard.

☐ MAKE SURE INSURANCE POLICY COVERS THE INTENDED CRUISING AREA.

☐ CARRY 'Q' FLAG AND COURTESY FLAGS FOR ANY COUNTRIES TO BE VISITED.

BEFORE
DEPARTURE

☐ CARRY OUT PRE-SAILING CHECK (See 13).

☐ CARRY OUT COMPLETE SAFETY EQUIPMENT CHECK (See 14).

☐ DRAW CREW'S ATTENTION TO CREW SAFETY CHECK (See 15).

SECTION 18   SPECIAL MAINTENANCE

The way to maintain certain items onboard
is self-evident - for instance deck gear
which needs greasing or painting. And
the procedure for looking after basic
items, such as batteries, is the same
regardless of the make or size of the
battery. But for some things like pumps,
winches, electric motors, electronic gear
etc, the maintenance instructions are
detailed by the manufacturer and may be
special to that piece of equipment.

In fact many items of modern marine
equipment have sealed units and need
little maintenance, often none at all,
although electrics thrive on regular use.
Sometimes, too, equipment is remarkably
tolerant of poor treatment, but the lack
of a few drops of oil once or twice a
year could well mean an embarrassing
breakdown and, possibly, the need for an
expensive replacement. The maintenance
needs of every item onboard should be
studies.

THE FOLLOWING PROCEDURE IS RECOMMENDED:
1.   LIST ANY ITEMS WHICH MAY NEED SPECIAL
     MAINTENANCE.   (See page 126).

☐ 2. ENSURE THAT THE RELEVANT HANDBOOKS, INSTRUCTION SHEETS ETC PROVIDED BY THE MANUFACTURER ARE AVAILABLE.

☐ 3. NOTE MAINTENANCE INSTRUCTIONS, IF ANY.

☐ 4. MAKE A PROGRAMME FOR CARRYING THEM OUT AND RECORD WHEN IT HAS BEEN DONE.

This procedure is less formidable than it sounds because, as has already been said, many items will be found to need no maintenance; but they must all be checked.

EXAMPLES OF ITEMS NEED- ING SPECIAL MAINTENANCE

The following are examples of equipment which may need special maintenance:

☐ SHEET AND HALYARD WINCHES

☐ BILGE PUMPS

☐ ROLLER REEFING GEAR

☐ FRESH WATER PUMP

☐ ANCHOR WINDLASS

☐ TOILETS

☐ OUTBOARD MOTORS

☐ RADAR

☐ POWER OR HAND DAVITS

☐ COOKING STOVES

☐ WINDSCREEN WIPERS

☐ TRIM TABS

☐ BOAT HEATERS

☐ STEERING GEAR

SECTION 19   LAYING UP

The details of a laying up programme will depend on whether the boat is to winter ashore or afloat. In particular, the extent to which engines, water systems, toilets etc are winterised will depend on climatic conditions. Nevertheless, the basic principles remain the same, regardless of circumstances.

Any work to be done by mechanics, boatyards, sailmakers etc should be put in hand as soon as the boat is laid up. In the case of a winter lay up, the spring rush will be avoided, work is likely to be carried out better, and may even be cheaper.

GENERAL ☐ DURING THE LAST CRUISE OF THE SEASON, OPERATE ALL EQUIPMENT (PUMPS, WINCHES, ELECTRONICS ETC), CHECK EVERY VALVE, TEST EVERY LIGHT, HAVE EVERY SAIL OUT OF ITS BAG. IT WILL THEN BE POSSIBLE TO MAKE A COMPREHENSIVE WORK LIST OF ANYTHING NEEDING ATTENTION DURING THE LAY UP PERIOD.

Section 19

GENERAL
(cont'd)

☐ THIS LIST SHOULD BE SUB-DIVIDED INTO:-
- WORK TO BE DONE BY OWNER OR CREW
- YARD OR OUTSIDE WORK
- ITEMS FOR PURCHASE OR RENEWAL

IT IS DESIRABLE AT THE SAME TIME TO
SEPARATE THE ITEMS WHICH ARE ESSENTIAL
FOR SAFETY OR SEAWORTHINESS.

☐ FILL DIESEL FUEL TANKS - UNLESS
CIRCUMSTANCES OF LAY UP MAKE THIS
UNDESIRABLE. This reduces chance of
condensation in tanks.

☐ CHECK INSURANCE FOR BOAT BEING LAID UP,
INCLUDING COVER FOR ANY GEAR THAT MAY BE
TAKEN HOME OR STOWED ELSEWHERE ASHORE.

☐ MAKE AN INVENTORY OF ALL GEAR REMOVED
FROM THE BOAT, INDICATING WHERE IT IS
STOWED OR WHERE TAKEN FOR REPAIR ETC.

☐ REMOVE ALL PORTABLE VALUABLES - BINOCULARS,
WATCHES, RADIOS ETC UNLESS THEY ARE
CONSIDERED TO BE SECURE ONBOARD.

☐ REMOVE BOTTLED GAS OR OTHER COOKING FUEL,
AND OUTBOARD MOTOR FUEL.

GENERAL
(cont'd)

☐ TOILETS - THOROUGHLY FLUSH THROUGH, THEN
CLOSE SEACOCKS AND WINTERISE IN ACCORDANCE
WITH MAKERS' INSTRUCTIONS. Stripping
toilets, cleaning and checking or renewing
valves and gaskets is well worth doing
each year. The job is not unpleasant if
toilets have been kept properly flushed.

☐ FRESH WATER SYSTEM - IF THERE IS DANGER OF
FREEZING, DRAIN SYSTEM INCLUDING PIPING
AND FRESH WATER PUMP.

☐ CLOSE ALL OTHER SEACOCKS. REMOVE ANY
RETRACTABLE LOG OR ECHO SOUNDER FITTINGS.

SAILS
AND
RIGGING

☐ INSPECT ALL SAILS FOR NEEDED REPAIRS.
SEND ASHORE TO SAILMAKER AND/OR LAUNDRY.

☐ UNREEVE RUNNING RIGGING. CHECK FOR WEAR
OR NEEDED REPAIRS. LABEL BEFORE STOWING.

IF MAST IS TO BE UNSTEPPED:

☐ - ELECTRIC MAST LEADS SHOULD BE LABELLED
TO ENSURE CORRECT RE-CONNECTION.

☐ - STANDING RIGGING TO BE LABELLED BEFORE
REMOVAL FROM MAST.

☐ - MAST SHOULD BE MARKED WITH YACHT'S NAME
BEFORE REMOVAL ASHORE.

Section 19

ENGINES
AND
GENERATORS ☐ CLOSE SEAWATER INTAKES, FLUSH COOLING
SYSTEMS WITH FRESH WATER, DRAIN AND
WINTERISE ACCORDING TO MAKERS' NOTES.

☐ CHECK RECOMMENDED MAINTENANCE SCHEDULES
AND COMPARE WITH ENGINE HOURS - PLAN ANY
ENGINE WORK THAT MAY BE NEEDED. It is
generally good sense to change engine oil
and lubricating oil filters, and fuel
filters during lay up period.

☐ WINTERISE OUTBOARDS IN ACCORDANCE WITH
MAKERS' INSTRUCTIONS.

ELECT-
RICAL ☐ BATTERIES - REMOVE ASHORE FOR CARE BY
YARD. Mark with boat's name.

☐ REMOVE BATTERIES FROM FLASHLIGHTS, RADIOS,
BUOYANT LIGHTS, AND ELECTRONIC EQUIPMENT.
SPRAY BATTERY CONNECTIONS WITH WD40 OR
SIMILAR.

☐ OPEN UP NAVIGATION LIGHTS AND OTHER DECK
ELECTRICAL FITTINGS: SPRAY WITH WD40 AND
CLOSE UP.

☐ COVERS OF ANY DECK SOCKETS (eg ANCHOR
LIGHTS) SHOULD BE GREASED TO MAKE THEM AS
WATERTIGHT AS POSSIBLE.

Section 19

EMERGENCY ☐ SEND LIFERAFT FOR ANNUAL SERVICING.
EQUIPMENT

☐ CHECK LIFEJACKETS AND SEND AWAY FOR
SERVICING IF NEEDED.

☐ FLARES - STOW IN DRY BUT AWAY FROM FIRE
RISK. CHECK EXPIRY DATE.

☐ LAND MEDICAL KIT FOR OVERHAUL (LEAVING
MINOR FIRST AID ITEMS FOR ANYONE WORKING
ONBOARD DURING THE LAY UP).

DOMESTIC ☐ REMOVE ALL FOOD FROM GALLEY, INCLUDING
DRY PROVISIONS AND CANNED GOODS.

☐ EMPTY ICE BOXES OR REFRIGERATORS. SCRUB
WITH DISINFECTANT AND LEAVE DOORS OPEN.

☐ SCRUB OUT ALL GALLEY LOCKERS AND DRAWERS,
CLEAN ALL GALLEY GEAR REMAINING ONBOARD.

☐ SCRUB OUT SHOWER AND TOILET COMPARTMENT
WITH DISINFECTANT.

Note: Even in a boat that is regularly
well kept, scrupulous cleanliness is
needed when leaving it unused for some
time in order to prevent mildew.

DOMESTIC
(cont'd)

☐ LAND ALL BLANKETS, SLEEPING BAGS, TOWELS, LINEN, ETC THAT NEED LAUNDERING OR DRY CLEANING.

☐ REMOVE ALL THOSE UNWANTED ITEMS THAT ACCUMULATE IN ALMOST ANY BOAT:
UNWANTED WIRE COATHANGERS
TORN FOUL WEATHER GEAR
OLD MAGAZINES
CLOTHING LEFT BY LAST SEASON'S GUESTS
UNLABELLED CANS OF FOOD
SHACKLES WITHOUT PINS ETC

VENTILATION

Efficient ventilation is essential in a boat that is laid up, not only to keep the atmosphere sweet and prevent mildew, but also to reduce the risk of rot.

☐ LEAVE ALL LOCKERS AND DRAWERS OPEN.

☐ REMOVE ENOUGH FLOOR BOARDS TO ALLOW A CURRENT OF AIR THROUGH THE BILGES.

☐ LEAVE AT LEAST ONE PORT OR VENT OPEN, IF THIS CAN BE DONE WITHOUT AFFECTING SECURITY OR LETTING IN THE RAIN.

☐ HAVE THE BOAT OPENED UP FOR AIRING AT REGULAR INTERVALS.

OWN BOAT DATA

Name...................... Type........................

Port of Registry.......... Official No................

LOA	LWL	Beam	Draft
......	......	....	....

Masthead height above waterline........................

Designer................... Builder....................

When and where built...................................

Classification............. Date of last survey.........

Signal letters............. Radio Call Sign.............

Tons displ	Tons gross	Tons net	Tons Thames
.....	.....	.....	......

Rating.................... Sail No....................

Berth/Mooring No...........

Notes...

....

....

....

....

OWN BOAT DATA   *Section 1 - DECK GEAR*

Anchors carried onboard

Type	Weight	Stowage
....	....	....
....	....	....
....	....	....
....	....	....

Anchor chain/line

Type	Size	Length
....	....	....
....	....	....
....	....	....
....	....	....

Markings on main anchor rode

....	....	....	....
....	....	....	....
....	....	....	....

Anchor winch/windlass

Make/model .... *Power supply* ....
Lubricant .... *Handle stowage* ....

OWN BOAT DATA   Section 2 - THE HULL

Seacocks and through-hull fittings. *Include all through-hull fittings, whether or not fitted with a seacock. Log and echo-sounder fittings should also be included.*

Position	Function	Type of Fitting
....	....	....
....	....	....
....	....	....
....	....	....
....	....	....
....	....	....

Stern glands, shaft bearings etc.

Where sited ....

Type of lubrication ....

Fresh water system.

Tanks position	Capacity	Filling position	Overflow
....	....	....	....
....	....	....	....

Changeover valves (if any) .... *Fresh water pump* ....

Bilge pumps

Type/make	Capacity	Where fitted	Strum Box
....	....	....	....
....	....	....	....

Wheel steering lubrication points ....

OWN BOAT DATA   _Section 3 - SAFETY AND EMERGENCY_
                           EQUIPMENT

Liferaft

Make......................... _Type_......................

Serial No.................... _Capacity_..........persons

Emergency pack contents.............................

....

Date of last service......... _Next service due_.........

Lifejackets

Make......................... _Type_......................

No. on board................. _Stowages_..................

Date last tested............. _Next test due_.............

Safety harnesses

_No_.......................... _Stowages_..................

Flares

Type	No	Stowage	Expiry date
....	......	....	....
....	......	....	....
....	......	....	....

First aid outfit/medical kit

Stowage................... _Contents last checked_........

Fire extinguishers

Type	Capacity	No	Stowage	Examined
....	....	.....	....	....
....	....	.....	....	....
....	....	.....	....	....

119

<u>OWN BOAT DATA</u> Section 4 - MECHANICAL

<u>Engine</u>

Make.................. Model.......... Year..........

Horsepower Max......... at.............. rpm

Max cont.............. at.............. rpm

Serial no.port........ stbd............

Fuel tank position(s)...................

Capacities ....

Regular engine oil.....

Sump capacity......... Oil filter No...................

Fuel filter type....... Fuel filter No.................

<u>Gearbox</u>

Make.................. Model.............

Serial number, port....

              stbd....

Ratio....... Oil type............... Capacity........

Any restrictions on trailing shaft.....................

Shaft diameter and material............................

Propeller diameter and pitch...........................

<u>Generator</u>

Make.................. Model.....................

Serial number.......... Capacity (kW)...................

Fuel filter No........ Oil filter No.................

Lube oil type......... Sump capacity..................

OWN BOAT DATA   *Section 5 - ELECTRICAL*

Standard voltage onboard ....
Items working on non-standard voltages ....
....
....

Batteries

Make ....
Date new ....
Voltage ....
Capacity (amp/hours) ....
Where sited ....

Battery charger

Make/Model ....
Voltages ....
Max charging rate ....

Fuseboards, Circuit breakers etc.

Where sited ....
....

Engine alternator

Make/Model ....
Voltage ....

Auxiliary generator

kW ....
Voltage ....

WARNING: *DO NOT SWITCH OFF BATTERY ISOLATING SWITCH*
           IF ALTERNATOR IS RUNNING, OR IT WILL BLOW.

OWN BOAT DATA   Section 6 - NAVIGATION AND RADIO

Steering Compass
Make............................ Serial No............
Date and place last swung ....
Echo sounder
Make/model ....
Serial number .... Power supply ....
Transducer sited .... Depth below water.....
Log/speedometer
Make .... Model ....
Serial number .... Power supply..........
Through-hull fitting ....
Radio
Make/model...................... Serial No ....
Type .... Output ....
Channels/frequency range ....
....
....
....
Antenna ....
Radar
Make/model .... Serial No ....
Scanner sited .... Power supply..........
R D F
Make/model .... Serial No ....
Type ....
Frequency range ....

OWN BOAT DATA   _INSURANCE_

Name and address of insurance company ....

....

....

Policy number........... _Where kept_.....................

Expiry date .... _Seasonal limitations_ ....

Geographical limits ....

....

....

Is cover adequate for boat (£........)

and third party (£........)?

OWN BOAT DATA   _LAST HAUL OUT_

Date and place ....

Paint/varnish	_Brand_	_Type_	_No of coats_
Anti-fouling	....	....	....
Boot topping	....	....	....
Topsides	....	....	....
Brightwork	....	....	....

Other work done ....

....

....

....

OWN BOAT DATA   Section 10 - SAILS AND RIGGING

Sail Inventory

Sail	Dimensions			Wt of cloth	Maker	Date
	Luff	Leech	Foot			

....
....
....
....
....
....
....
....
....
....
....
....

Headsail sheeting positions

....
....
....
....
....
:...

Standing and running rigging -- Sizes and Materials

	Constr.	Dia.	Material
Shrouds Upper			
Shrouds Lower			
Shrouds Inter			
Forestay			
Babystay			
Backstay			
Running backstay			
Main halyard			
Jib/genoa halyard			
Spin halyard			
Mizzen halyard			
Spin foreguys			
Main sheet			
Jib sheet			
Spin sheets			
Mizzen sheet			
Spin guys			

SPECIAL MAINTENANCE SCHEDULE

Item	Maker's Instructions Available?	Maintenance required
. . . .		
. . . .		
. . . .		
. . . .		
. . . .		
. . . .		
. . . .		
. . . .		
. . . .		
. . . .		
. . . .		

INVENTORY OF VALUABLE ITEMS

Item	Make	Serial No.	Remarks
. . . .			
. . . .			
. . . .			
. . . .			
. . . .			
. . . .			
. . . .			
. . . .			
. . . .			
. . . .			

BIBLIOGRAPHY

Adlard Coles Ltd

Care of Alloy Spars and Rigging - Potter

Care and Repair of Hulls - Verney

Care and Repair of Sails - Howard-Williams

Care and Repair Below Decks - Blandford

Care and Repair of Marine Petrol Engines - Goring

Care and Repair of Small Diesel Engines - Thompson

Fitting Out, Maintenance and Repair of Small Craft -
  Sleightholme

Electrical and Electronic Equipment for Yachts - French

Nautical Publishing

Boat Maintenance - Ideas and Practice - Jones

Practical Points on Boat Engines - Donat

Owning a Boat - Marriott

Pelham

Encyclopaedia of Small Craft Maintenance - Blandford

David and Charles

Boat Engines - Bowyer

Bodley Head

Small Boat Skipper's Handbook - Lewis

DTI

How Safe is Your Craft?

INDEX